GEORGE HERBERT
From Donne's *Lives* (1675 ed.)
By permission of the Bodleian Library (Bod. Vet.A3.f. 1642)

GEORGE HERBERT
A PORTRAIT

by
Nick Page

MONARCH
Tunbridge Wells

Copyright © Nick Page 1993
The right of Nick Page to be identified
as author of this work has been asserted by him in
accordance with the Copyright, Design
and Patents Act 1988

First published 1993

ISBN 1 85424 180 X

British Library Cataloguing in Publication Data
A catalogue record for this book is available
from the British Library.

Production and Printing in England for
MONARCH PUBLICATIONS
P.O. Box 163, Tunbridge Wells, Kent TN3 0NZ by
Nuprint Ltd, Station Road, Harpenden, Herts AL5 4SE

CONTENTS

THIS BOOK, about a man and his brothers, is dedicated to my own brother David, with thanks for his love, friendship and support.

1

July 1627

Chelsea

'A PIECE OF A CHURCHYARD FITTS EVERY BODY.'
Outlandish Proverbs No.1027

A Memorial Service

On Sunday 1 July 1627, a young man travelled from his lodgings in central London to the small but prosperous village of Chelsea.

He was a businessman, a merchant of the City of London, and his journey that day took him west from his lodgings near Fleet Street, through Temple Bar (the western gate of the City proper) and past the palaces and sumptuous dwellings lining the Strand, with their gardens rolling down to the banks of the Thames. At the village of Charing, now very much a suburb of the City, the roads forked, heading north to St Giles or South West, through Westminster and the fields and market gardens beyond, eventually arriving at Chelsea.

He was travelling to attend a church service—not an ordinary Sunday service, but a service of commemoration for a woman who had died in the previous month. Aside from her reputation, he did not know the lady personally, and it was not an act of homage that had drawn him there. Instead he had come more as a fan, for he wanted to hear the preacher, in whose parish he lived and with whom he was well acquainted.

> Oh Eternal and most Glorious God, who sometimes in thy Justice, dost give the dead bodies of the Saints to be meat unto the Fowles of the Heaven and the flesh of thy Saints unto the beasts of the Earth . . .[1]

As the preacher prayed before the sermon, his words hinted

9

that this was no mere job of work; he was clearly emotionally attached to the woman he was about to eulogise. In an age where it was no disgrace for men to display their emotions, the priest made no attempt to conceal the debt he owed this woman, for he had known the lady a long time, and had spent much time in her company. He had written poems to her and exchanged witty letters. She had even sheltered him at her house in Chelsea during one of the bouts of plague that had emptied London in the previous years. In his early days, when he had been struggling to support his wife and seven children, she had 'prov'd one of his most bountiful Benefactors'.[2]

His text for the sermon was taken from 2 Peter 3:13: 'Nevertheless, we, according to his promises, looke for new heavens, and new earth, wherein dwelleth righteousnesse.' He began:

> I propose to my selfe and to this Congregation, two
> Workes for this day; That wee may walke together two
> miles, in this Sabbath daies journey; First, To instruct the
> Living, and then To commemorate the Dead. Which
> office, as I ought, so I should have performed sooner, but
> that this sad occasion surprized me under other Pre-
> obligations and Pre-contracts, in the services of mine own
> Profession which could not be excused nor avoided.[3]

As he listened to the sermon, the visitor's eyes no doubt wandered among the congregation. He saw the deceased woman's husband sitting up at the front – a handsome, distinguished-looking man, and yet surprisingly young, almost as young as some of the woman's sons who were sitting near him. Clearly there had been a considerable difference in their ages, a fact which had caused much gossip at the time of their betrothal. They were local residents, and lived in a house near to the church, where he had laid out a famous Italian garden.

Then there were her sons and daughters. The eldest son was a big, bluff, black-haired, good-looking fellow with pointed black beard and sharp, angry eyes. His younger brother was different entirely; he was thin and pale and looked ill. Long, lank hair hung straight down on either side of his high forehead. His sharp, almost pointed nose and high cheekbones gave his face a lean and cadaverous look.

Other members of the family were in attendence, for she had

given birth to ten children by her previous husband. Perhaps one of the best-known of them was the Master of the Revels, the licenser and censor of all the plays for which London was so noted, and a man who had profited greatly from the fees he pocketed for his work.

> And, as she ever hastned her family and her company
> hither, with that cheerful provocation: *For God's sake let's*
> *go, for God's sake let's bee there at the Confession;* So her
> selfe with her whole family... did, every Sabbath, shut up
> the day, at night, with a generall, with a cheerful singing of
> Psalmes...'[4]

The sermon, after a long first half concentrating on the day of judgement and the need to have faith in a future life, now moved on to a more direct commemoration of the woman who lay buried in a tomb near them. Perhaps the visitor's attention switched to the church itself. The furnishings though familiar were still, in these turbulent times, the subject of arguments and controversy. There were within the English Church factions arguing for subtle changes, taking the church back towards its Catholic roots. Then there were others, the sterner, Puritan elements who rejected the fancies and fripperies of the High Church for an altogether more austere worship. Most churchgoers, as the preacher was now affirming, walked the safe middle path:

> And, her rule for her particular understanding of the
> Scripture was the Church. Shee never diverted towards the
> Papist in undervaluing the Scripture; nor towards the
> Separatist in undervaluing the Church. But in the doctrine
> and discipline of that Church, in which, God seal'd her, to
> himselfe, in Baptisme, shee brought up her children, shee
> assisted her family, shee dedicated her soule to God in her
> life, and surrendered it to him in her death; And in that
> forme of Common Prayer, which is ordain'd by that
> Church, and to which she had accustom'd her selfe with
> her family, twice every day, she joyn'd with that company
> which was about her death-bed, in answering to every part
> thereof, which the Congregation is directed to answer to,
> with a cleere understanding, with a constant memmory,
> with a distinct voyce, not two houres before she died.[5]

Here, then, was a woman of her times. A woman of the English Church, of the *via media*. Neither leaning too much towards Rome, nor towards Geneva. A woman who kept her head and her faith, a model Christian in this 'time of jestes and profane wit'. And so the sermon, garnished with a few more compliments, drew to its close.

A service of commemoration was, of course, no more unusual in the seventeenth century than it is today; indeed, in many ways Jacobean society was more used to death than we are. Death was something that every family experienced, not something cold and alien and restricted to hospital corridors.

There were, however, several factors that made this particular service significant. One was that it was commemorating the life of Magdalene Danvers, wife of Sir John Danvers. Another was that the congregation included many notable members, such as Lord Edward Herbert, and his brother Henry Herbert, Master of the Revels. The preacher was none other than John Donne, one-time poet and rake, now Dean of St Paul's. And the thin, ill-looking son was George Herbert, Orator of Cambridge University. Only a few weeks later this service would be enshrined in print in a pamphlet comprising the text of Donne's sermon and a series of Latin and Greek verses written by George in commemoration of his mother.

Perhaps the main reason that this service is of such significance is that it was the only time all these characters were brought together with the man who was to make many of them famous. For the visitor who travelled that afternoon to hear Dr Donne preach was eventually to write biographies of both Donne and George Herbert. His name was Izaak Walton.

If there is one man responsible for creating the image of George Herbert as some kind of Anglican saint, it is Walton. This service was the only time in his life he laid eyes on George Herbert. In its own way, however, it was the beginning of a lifetime's relationship.

London

'THERE ARE MANY WAIES TO FAME.'
Outlandish Proverbs No.539

Walton's *Life of Herbert*

It is impossible to write about George Herbert without falling under the shadow of the observer at that church service so long ago.

Izaak Walton's *Life of Mr. George Herbert* was first published in 1670, thirty-seven years after the poet and clergyman had died. In between the two events, George Herbert had become a best-seller. His posthumously published book of poems, *The Temple*, had gone through nine editions. Indeed, Walton estimated that it had sold over 20,000 copies in the forty years since publication– this in an age where books were expensive and where even such a blockbuster as *Paradise Lost* only sold 3,000 copies in its first eleven years.[1]

His life as a priest at Bemerton and the subject matter of his poetry had secured for Herbert a holy and pious reputation. Even his brother, with perhaps a hint of sarcasm, wrote in his auto-biography that George's life 'was most holy and exemplary, in so much that about Salisbury where he lived...he was little less than Sainted'.[2]

If, for his brother, Herbert was a little less than sainted, then others wanted to make sure that deficiency was quickly made up. Successive divines and poets took a similar view to that of Richard Codrington, who wrote in 1638:

> View a true Poet, whose bare lines
> Include more goodnesse then some shrines.

Wee'le canonize him, and what er
Befalls, style him heauens Chorister.'[3]

A few years after these verses were written Britain was torn
apart by rebellion and conflict, much of which had been inspired
by religious issues. Walton saw Herbert as a paradigm of pre-
revolutionary Anglican piety, living proof that the true English
Church was one of ritual and decorous liturgy; not that of the
Commonwealth, but of the Restoration. To Walton, therefore,
Herbert was not so much a subject, as a cause. If he could prove
that Herbert was both a saint and a fully paid-up Anglo Catholic,
then he could rest his case.

He did his job so well that even today, when much of Walton's
work has been discredited, the myth of 'saintly George Herbert'
still lingers. 'Unlike most of us, [George Herbert] was a saint',
says one recent biographical sketch. Three centuries after its first
publication, the myth of George Herbert shows no signs of running out of steam.[4]

Of course, it is perfectly acceptable for Walton to hold such
theories—every biographer has theories about his subject. What is
less acceptable is that Walton altered the facts to fit. His *Life of
Herbert* is beautifully written, fascinating, moving, funny and
poignant. It is also inaccurate. Facts are confused, conversations
are made up, stories invented. To convince the jury of his case, he
tampered with the evidence.

He would not have necessarily believed that he was doing
anything wrong. We must be careful not to condemn Walton for
failing to hit a target at which he was not even aiming. He was not
trying to write a 'biography' as we understand the term. He was
trying to create a parable.

In the end, however, such tampering has had just the opposite
effect to that which he desired. In the general horror and tut-
tutting over Walton's economy with the truth, there has been a
rush to the opposite extreme; to the belief that his entire concep-
tion of Herbert's life was wrong.

Walton's thesis is that Herbert was a brilliant, well-educated,
and noble gentleman, who, when his court hopes were dashed,
turned to the Anglican Church where he found fulfilment, honour
and respect. The anti-Waltonists, however, reject the idea that
Herbert even notionally considered the fripperies of the secular

life. To them, Herbert knew almost from the start what he was going to do; his career path was an ineluctable path to the priesthood.

To use a proverb that Herbert would have liked, they have thrown the baby out with the bathwater. Their theories have as many holes as Walton's. If, for example, Herbert really intended to enter the church, why did he leave it so late? Why did he prevaricate instead of becoming priest at the earliest possible opportunity? Why indeed, did he bother with the academic and courtly life at all?

Walton has certainly tampered with the decoration, but that does not mean we have to condemn the whole building. After all, no biographer, however talented, can completely reverse the tenor of a man's life. The job of a propagandist is to exaggerate characteristics that are already there—to make heroes more heroic and villains more villainous. The job of any modern biographer of Herbert is not to reject Walton entirely, but to sift the facts and weigh the probabilities.

Both Walton and his opponents have something to offer us. Beneath his distortions, Walton is fundamentally right; Herbert was intelligent, able and apparently set for a life of honour and patronage; he did attempt to seek court preferment; and failing that, he did choose the relative obscurity of a tiny Wiltshire village. At the same time, the anti-Walton camp is correct to point out that George had certainly considered the priesthood early in his career, that he rejected his court hopes before they rejected him and that he was not the High Churchman that Walton would have us believe him to be.

The truth is, of course, somewhere between the two. George Herbert tried to marry the spiritual with the secular—only to discover that such a relationship inevitably ends with divorce. He was certain that God had called him, but the exact nature of that call was, for many reasons, hard for him to accept. God sometimes calls us to that which we view with both desire and dislike, desire because it accords with what we want in our hearts, dislike because it takes us away from exciting and often more comfortable alternatives. Our tendency then is, like Jonah, to decide not to decide, to head in the opposite direction, hoping by success in other fields to persuade God that he was wrong—even though, deep down, we know that he was right. George Herbert was

indeed a saint, but in the true sense. He was a member of the
church, a follower of Christ, and like all such saints, he wrestled
with conflicting desires and struggled to submit his will to the will
of God. In the end he succeeded, but it was a long and hard-
fought contest.

> 'IN EVERY ART IT IS GOOD TO HAVE A MASTER.'
> Outlandish Proverbs No.619

Background and Sources

This book is not only about George Herbert, but also about his
family. I have included such details not only for the light they
throw on the poet himself, but because they are interesting in
themselves. If there are two people I have concentrated on particularly, they are his mother Magdalene and his elder brother
Edward. Both had a marked effect on George's life, opinions and
actions and both deserve biographies of their own. I have also
included historical information about the time in which George
Herbert lived. It was not my intention to write a popular history
of the early seventeenth century, but I thought it safer to assume
my readers unfamiliar with the major events of the time.

With regard to major sources, they are noted in the bibliogra-
phy. Along with Walton's *Life*, however, three other major
sources deserve particular mention.

Firstly, the standard edition of George Herbert's poetry and
prose is Hutchinson's complete *Works*, published in 1941 and
amended in 1945. Where Herbert's writings are quoted they are
invariably taken from this edition. With regard to the poetry, this
is not a book of literary criticism. I have attempted to examine the
poems for the light they shed on Herbert himself. Matters of
style, structure and poetic image I have largely left to the experts.

Secondly, I have had much recourse to Amy Charles' *A Life of
George Herbert*, published in 1977. This remarkably thorough
book contains detailed analysis of virtually every piece of evidence
associated with George Herbert. Though I have differed with
Professor Charles on many points, every Herbert scholar is per-
petually in her debt for the care, intelligence and meticulous
attention to detail which she brought to bear in her book.

Thirdly, along with poems, histories and books of philosophy,

George's brother Edward Herbert left behind him an autobiography. Critical opinion of this book has varied.[5] Horace Walpole, when he first read it, 'could not get on for laughing and screaming' and when he published the first edition it was because he thought it a fund of unconscious and unintended humour.[6] This view of Edward as a seventeenth-century Don Quixote endured for many years, although recent critics have attempted a re-evaluation. Edward certainly appears foolish at times. His adventures are often farcical and his insistence on the joys of duelling strike one as eccentric in the extreme. However, despite the disappointments of his life, his book is never bitter or vindictive. The *Life of Edward Herbert, Lord Cherbury* (1764) is sometimes vague, occasionally funny and frequently moving. Above all it is a rigorously honest account of a man's life by one to whom the truth meant more than it ever meant to Walpole or some of the critics who were to follow.

3

Montgomery

'THE BEST SMELL IS BREAD, THE BEST SAVOUR, SALT, THE
BEST LOVE THAT OF CHILDREN.'
Outlandish Proverbs No.741

Birth in Montgomery

George Herbert was born on 3 April 1593 in the family seat at
Montgomery, Wales.

Writing some fifty years earlier, the antiquary John Leland had
recorded that Montgomery:

> ...Standithe a mile from Severn banke, and is servid with
> small rills cominge frome the hills hard by. The soyle of
> the ground of the towne is on mayne slaty roke, and
> especially the parte of the towne hillinge toward the castell,
> now a-late reedified, whereby hathe bene a parke. Great
> ruines of the waulle yet apere *ad vestigia* of iiii gates thus
> cawlyd, Kedewen Gate, Chyrbyry Gate, Artur's Gate,
> Kery Gate. In the waulls yet remayne broken towrets, of
> the wiche the whit towre is now moste notable. One
> paroche churche in Mountgomerike. There liethe a good
> plentifull valley by the towne of corne and grace.[1]

In Leland's time the castle may well have been 'a-late
reedified', but by the time of George's birth it was run-down and
Walton's statement that, 'The place of his Birth was near to the
Town of *Montgomery*, and in that *Castle* that did then bear the
name of that Town and County...'[2] is unlikely to be accurate.

A survey taken by one 'Rob't Lloid' in January 1593 deals with
the 'decaes of the said Castell...' and gives an outline of the

general dereliction of the family seat: 'There ys noe housholde stuffe in the Castell but onlie a brassen boyling potte ijo sesterns of leadd & one lyttle peece of waynscotte remayninge in the grett hall or dyning Chamber'.[3] If this report is accurate, the castle can scarcely have been habitable three months later when George was born. Indeed, it remained in a state of disrepair until 1621 when Edward Herbert, George's elder brother built a new brick house in the lower bailey of the medieval structure.[4]

George was probably born in the town of Montgomery itself, where the family lived in a long, low building called Black Hall, which was built sometime after 1560. Occupation seems to have been short-lived and probably ended by 1618. The house was apparently part of an extensive estate including gardens and orchards. The hall was within the town walls in the north-eastern corner of Montgomery, at the place now known as Plas Du. Thomas Pennant's *Tour in Wales* (1780) records the local tradition that Black Hall was 'consumed by fire'.[5]

The house was built by George's grandfather Edward, who established a reputation for hospitality and good food. His grandson and namesake Edward wrote:

> He delighted also much in Hospitality, as having a very long Table twice covered every Meal with the best Meats that could be gotten, and a very great Family. It was an ordinary saying in the countrey at that time, when they saw any Fowl rise, fly where thou wilt thou wilt light at Black Hall, which was a low Building, but of great capacity, my Grand-Father erected in his Age; his Father and Himself in former times having lived in Montgomery castle.[6]

'RIVERS NEEDE A SPRING.'
Outlandish Proverbs No.600

Ancestry and Family

The family into which George was born was a notable one. Descended from a companion of William the Conqueror, the Herberts had gradually risen through the ranks of the nobility until in the fifteenth century they were prominent landowners and gentry in the border regions of Wales. They first became the

Herberts around 1460, when William Herbert, later created Earl of Pembroke, adopted the English system of family names, in preference to the Welsh system favoured by his father Sir William ap Thomas. The family into which George was born was descended from the first Earl's brother, Sir Richard Herbert.[7]

At the time of George's birth, the Manor was in the hands of Sir Richard's grandson–and George's grandfather–Sir Edward Herbert. Sir Edward, who was born in 1513 or 1514, was a figure of much power and influence in the area. After his father's death in 1541 he became Constable of Montgomery Castle, to which he added the title Lord Chirbury in 1553. He also served as Sheriff and Member of Parliament for the county. Indeed, so attached was he to the service of Parliament that towards the end of his long life he overcame his advancing years to defeat his brother-in-law Arthur Price of Newport and gain election as Knight of the Shire for Montgomery.

It was his activities as a courtier and soldier that really laid the foundations for the family fortunes. During his long and active life, Sir Edward was Squire of the Body to Queen Elizabeth and a soldier of renown.[8] According to his grandson, the grandfather of George Herbert made his reputation and his fortune with his sword at St Quentin in France and in battles during the reigns of Edward IV and Mary.[9]

Certainly in the local area he was a figure of some stature, both physically and symbolically. As Edward wrote:

> My Grand-Father was noted to be a great enemy to the Outlaws and Thieves of his time, who robbed in great numbers in the Mountains in Montgomeryshire, for the suppressing of whom he went often both day and night to the places where they were.[10]

Such forays opened him to all manner of dangers:

> Some Outlaws being lodged in an Alehouse upon the hills of Llandinam, my Grand-Father and a few servants coming to apprehend them, the Principal Outlaw shot an Arrow against my Grandfather which stuck in the Pummel of his Sadle, whereupon my Grandfather coming up to him with his sword in his hand, and taking him Prisoner, he showed him the said arrow, bidding him look what he had done,

whereof the Outlaw was no farther sensible than to say he
was sorry that he left his better bow at home which he
conceiv'd would have carryed his shot to his Body, but the
Outlaw being brought to Iustice, suffer'd for it.[11]

Sir Edward lived to the ripe old age of eighty, dying only six
weeks or so after the birth of his grandson George.

George's father Richard was also a man of bravery and physical
courage, which on at least one occasion resulted in severe physical
injury:

> He chaced his adversaries untill a Villain coming behind
> him did over the shoulders of others wound him on the
> head behind with a forest Bill until he fell down, though
> recovering himself again, notwithstanding his skull was
> cutt through to the Pia Mater of the Brain...[12]

Although he recovered from this bout, it may well have been
such injuries that led to Richard's early death, for he lived only a
further three-and-a-half years, dying in 1596. Like his father
before him (and his sons in their turn) he served in Parliament, as
well as serving as Sheriff of Montgomery, Magistrate for the
County and *Custos Rotulorum* (the officer charged with keeping
the records of the courts in a county). He was an educated man,
'His Learning was not vulgar, as understanding well the Latin
Tongue, and being well versed in history.'[13]

Richard was remembered by his son Edward as 'black haired
and bearded, as all my Ancestors of his side are said to have been,
of a manly or somewhat stern look, but withall very handsome
and well compact in his Limbs'.[14] This 'black haired and bearded
look' was, indeed, characteristic of the family, seen notably in
Edward himself. Richard's early death – probably while he was in
his forties – exhibits another, more unfortunate family characteristic.

'THE GOOD MOTHER SAYES NOT, WILL YOU? BUT GIVES.'
Outlandish Proverbs No.467

Magdalene Herbert

George Herbert's mother was a beautiful woman. She was the
youngest daughter of Richard Newport, who died in 1570 leaving
a dowry of £200 to be paid one year after her marriage, or
whenever after marriage she reached the age of twenty. As the
fourth daughter, her chances of marrying would normally have
been slim, but due to this generous dowry her mother had been
able to arrange an advantageous match. She married Richard
Herbert in 1581 at the Newport family home at Eyton-upon-
Severn, Shropshire.[15]

Perhaps another reason why she attracted such an eligible
match was her undoubted beauty and, if future years are anything
to go by, her wit and intelligence. Throughout her life, Magdalene Herbert was renowned as a woman of virtue, piety, charity
and beauty. Their first years of marriage were divided between
Black Hall and Magdalene's mother at Eyton. They were at Eyton
when their first son, Edward was born.

'ONE FATHER IS MORE THEN A HUNDRED SCHOOLMASTERS.'
Outlandish Proverbs No.686

Edward Herbert

Edward's autobiography, written when he was well advanced in
years, is an absorbing account of his life and times, centred
mainly around his military and amorous exploits. Always
delightfully, if infuriatingly, vague he could never recall the date
and year of his birth (although he is specific about the place and
the time). Given that his sister Elizabeth was born in November
1583, it is impossible that Edward could have been born on 3
March 1583, so it seems likely he was born the year before in
1582.[16]

Edward like others in his family was a boy of delicate health, at
least for the first few years of his life. 'My Infancy was very sickly
my hed continualy purging it selfe very much by the Eares,
wherevpon also It was soe long before I began to speake That

many thought I should bee euer dumbe'.[17] He spent most of the years of his childhood at Eyton-upon-Severn, where his education suffered because of his illness, 'I remember this defluction at my Eares... continued in that Uiolence That my Freinds did not think fitt to teach mee soe much as my Alphabett, till I was seauen yeare old at what tyme my defluction Ceased...'[18]

Edward was born in 1582. In the fifteen years of their marriage, Magdalene gave birth to seven boys and three girls. Edward was followed by Elizabeth in 1583, then Margaret (born c. 1585), Richard (born c. 1587), William (March 1589 or 90), Charles (c. 1592), George (3 April 1593), Henry (June or July 1594), Frances (c. 1595) and the youngest son, Thomas (born May 1597) after the death of his father.

There are no baptism records for George, but it may well be that he was baptised privately, especially if he was an ailing child.

When he was fourteen, Edward went to university (although with typical inaccuracy, or perhaps a bit of bragging, he recalled going to university at the age of twelve). Whatever his age, he had not been there many months when the news came to him of his father's illness:

> I had not beene many moneths in the Vniuersity but news was brought mee of my Fathers death, his Sicknes being a Lethargie Caros or Coma uigilans which continued long vpon him; he seemed at last to dye without much paine though in his Senses. Vpon opinion giuen by Phisitians That his disease was mortall my Mother thought fit to send for mee home.[19]

Richard died in October 1596. Few of his children were old enough at the time of his death to remember much of their father. Certainly George, aged only three-and-a-half, could only have had the sketchiest of memories.

The death of her husband caused immediate problems for Magdalene. Not only was she two months pregnant, but Edward was still a minor, which raised questions about the estate. Her husband had died either intestate or inadequately advised, having in the words of Edward, 'made either noe will or such an imperfect one, that it was not proved'.[20] This was not unusual, for many left the drawing of the will until the last possible moment.

Perhaps Richard, only fitfully conscious between bouts of coma, simply left it too late.

The only evidence we have for what the contents of his will would have been is the assertion of his wife that one of his wishes was to leave an annuity of £40 each for his younger sons and dowries for each of his three daughters. When Edward came of age she ensured that he respected these wishes—or she tried to ensure it, for these annuities were the cause of constant anxiety and frustration for the younger brothers: throughout his life, Edward was notoriously reluctant to pay up.[21]

As there was no will for probate, Magdalene Herbert had to take other steps. Initially, she applied for an administration award, which was granted to her and her son Edward on 3 May 1597. She then took steps to secure her own rents and incomes by purchasing her marriage licence from the Court of Wards and Liveries for £40.[22]

The main priority, however, was to secure the wardship of her eldest son:

> My Mother thought fitt to send for mee home, And presently after my Fathers death to desire her Brother Sir Francis Newport to hastèn to London to obtayne my wardshippe for his and her vse joyntly, which hee obtayned.[23]

The process, however, was by no means as simple as Edward makes out. Wardships were a profitable business in the sixteenth century, especially for the Crown. Henry VIII had established the Court of Wards in 1540 partly as a means of establishing his feudal rights over his landowners. Heirs or heiresses who were minors, as well as widows and the insane, came automatically under the jurisdiction of the Court of Wards, who administered their lands and estates and could even arrange their marriage or remarriage. However, a payment could ensure the grant of a wardship to a third party (as well as adding to the Crown's coffers).[24]

Newport would have had to visit numerous officials and prepare documents. In the end it appears he took expert advice from Sir George More of Losely Park. Sir George was the Keeper of the

Tower and was later to become, albeit rather unwittingly, the father-in-law of John Donne.

'IF YOU MUST FLIE, FLIE WELL.'
Outlandish Proverbs No.1021

First Moves

Once the wardship was secured, Magdalene Herbert moved her household to Eyton-upon-Severn. No doubt the security offered by her family home would have been very welcome at this difficult time, especially since she had just given birth to Richard's last child, christened Thomas at the baptism service on 15 May 1597.

It was to be the first of several moves. Magdalene Herbert took very seriously her responsibility to look after the family following the death of her husband, and at least one of the moves can be seen as a desire to provide for and support the education of her children. Yet there is a paradox here. The best way of protecting her children would have been to remarry; yet Magdalene did not do so for many years.

In her moves, there is almost a feeling of freedom, of release. After all, she could have remained in Montgomery. Equally she could have settled with the family in Eyton. Instead, she went to centres of culture and activity–to Oxford and then to London, places where she soon established a reputation of her own. She was no longer Sir Richard's wife, bearing baby after baby in the obscure country town of Montgomery. Instead she became the woman fêted by Donne in his poetry. Perhaps there was a sense in which the death of her husband actually brought out the best in this resourceful and intelligent woman. Perhaps Magdalene Herbert saw an opportunity, if not for escape, then at least for individual fulfilment.

So when the family left Montgomery in 1597, for Magdalene at least, it was a final parting. If she ever went back, it can only have been for the briefest of spells. In more ways than one, she had moved on.

4

Eyton-Upon-Severn, Oxford

'A GREAT DOWRY IS A BED FULL OF BRABLES.'
Outlandish Proverb No.758

Edward's Marriage

When the family left Montgomery, George Herbert was only four. His earliest memories would therefore have been of upheaval, of the turmoil caused by his father's death, and of the journeying that began after that. The upheaval must have been considerable, for the household was a considerable size; along with Magdalene herself, there were the ten children–beginning with Edward (aged fourteen) and extending down to baby Thomas. No doubt there would also have been family servants and nurses.

Edward was fourteen and attending Oxford University. This was by no means an unusual age for an undergraduate, as we shall see when we come to examine George's university career. Sending one's children to university was still a relatively new idea for gentry, but the Herbert family had always been keen on learning. Edward had a tutor for some years before matriculating at Oxford, and had already made quick progress in Greek, Latin and logic. He entered Oxford in May 1596 only a few months before the death of his father.[1] Whether he returned to Oxford in the intervening period between Richard's death and the family's move to Oxford is unknown. What is certain is that securing her sons' wardship was not enough for Magdalene. Her desire to secure the future prosperity of her family (and especially of Edward) led her to add to the already large family by arranging the marriage of her eldest son.

Edward was still three days short of his sixteenth birthday

when, on 28 February 1598 he married his cousin, Mary Herbert, daughter of Sir William Herbert of St Julians.

It was a strange affair. In his will, Sir William had stipulated that his daughter could only marry someone with the surname 'Herbert'. If she chose to marry another, most of his lands in Monmouthshire and Ireland would descend to another branch of the Herbert family and Mary and her husband would be left with a much smaller parcel of land in Anglesey and Caernarvonshire.[2] Sir William had died in 1592. In the six years since his death, no Herbert had come forward to claim his daughter.

To Magdalene, the marriage must have seemed the ideal solution. Despite the fact that at twenty-one the bride was five years older than the husband, the lands would more than make up for it, for they were worth some £30,000.[3] It was perhaps the most convenient marriage of convenience that she could have desired.

Unfortunately for Edward, Magdalene had not investigated well enough. For Sir William's lands were heavily mortgaged and nowhere near the value they should have been. The result was that Edward's arranged marriage did not secure for him the riches it promised. He found himself tied to a woman several years older than him, without even the consolation of great wealth. Small wonder that throughout his life he seemed to view his wife as some kind of sexual relief, rather than as a companion. Initially, all his marriage achieved was to turn him back to his learning. 'Having a due remedy for that Lasciviousnes to which youth is naturally inclined, I followed my booke more close then euer...' he wrote.[4]

Perhaps this failed arrangement was the beginning of the coolness between Edward and his mother that was only to increase as the years went by. In his autobiography he writes admiringly of his younger brother Henry: 'By a good marriage he attained to great fortunes, for himself and posterity to enjoy.' It was the good marriage that Edward had signally failed to achieve, the marriage for which his mother was to blame.

Her failure was further emphasised, at least in Edward's mind, by the arrangements of his maternal grandmother. Margaret Bromley Newport died within a year of her eldest grandson's marriage. Unlike her son-in-law, however, she had prepared a perfectly good will. What is more, the will left provision for

Edward. Years later, he wrote admiringly of Margaret Newport, that in remaining a widow and not remarrying she was

> ...So carefull to provide for her Posterity that though it were in her power to give her Estate (which was very great) to whom she would, yet she continued still unmarried, and so provident for them, that...she deliver'd up her Estate and care of housekeeping to her eldest Son Francis...[5]

The inference is clear. Margaret Newport had remained a widow and had left a proper inheritance for her eldest son. Magdalene Herbert, as we shall see, did neither of these things. Throughout his autobiography, Edward withholds such admiration for his mother, and, most notably, completely fails to mention her remarriage.

'HE THAT GOETH FARRE HATH MANY ENCOUNTERS.'
Outlandish Proverbs No.608

Move to Oxford

There can be no doubt that the breach between the mother and her son was not helped by the character of Edward himself. The reference to the appetites of the young shows that he was no slow developer. At sixteen he had all the glowering good looks, wit and intelligence of an ideal courtier. Unfortunately he also had a hair-trigger temper, and a pile of chips on his shoulder. He was a fiery character, prone to bouts of anger and intemperate language; as quick to pick a fight as he was to flirt with the ladies. Such characteristics must have caused his mother great concern, so much so that when the time came for Edward to return to Oxford, the family moved with him. The move was to some extent pre-cipitated by Margaret Newport's death, but it was also to allow Magdalene to keep an eye on her volatile son. Although his marriage had removed one particular danger, like so many six-teen-year-olds before and after, Edward was still an accident waiting to happen.

Before she left Eyton, however, Magdalene paid her final respects to her dead husband by arranging for the erection of a splendid monument to him (and her) in the church where he was buried. To a certain extent she was following family practice—both her parents and grandparents had been commemorated by such tombs at Wroxeter.[6]

The tomb at Montgomery is a magnificent affair—the two recumbent figures of Magdalene and Richard Herbert lie beneath a vaulted canopy, while behind them kneel images of six sons and two daughters. The figures of the children are not intended to be accurate representations, no attempt having been made to distinguish between their ages. They are not portraits but decorations.

The inscription reads:

> Heare Lieth the Body of Richard Herbert Esquire Whose Monument was Made at the Cost of Magdalene his Wife Daughter to Sr Richard Newport of Highe Arcall in the County of Salop Knighte (deceased) & of Dame Margaret his Wife Daughter & Sole Heire to Sr Thomas Bromley Late Lord Chiefe Justice of England & one of the Executors of the Late Kinge of Most Famous Memorie Kinge Henry the Eighte ANO DOM 1600.[7]

For what was supposed to be a monument to Richard there is a surprising amount of information about Magdalene and her family. Perhaps the church was already full enough of memorials to the Herbert family. Despite the fact that the monument was made 'at the Cost' of Magdalene, there is no evidence she ever returned to Montgomery to see the result of her expense. The fact that she included herself in the monument indicates she expected to be buried there, but even this did not come to fruition: she is buried in Chelsea.

Magdalene probably moved to Oxford in 1599. Edward recalls that 'Not long after my mariag I went againe to Oxford together with my wife and Mother who tooke a house and lived for a certayne tyme there.'[8]

Oxford at the time was an expanding city. Although the great wave of expansion would not come until later in the new century with the foundation of Wadham College and Pembroke College, and the remodelling of Jesus, Lincoln and Exeter Colleges, when Edward arrived Sir Thomas Bodley was just beginning his work on the decayed and decrepit Duke Humphrey's library, which would transform it into the Bodleian.

Visitors were generally struck by the air of tranquillity and calmness about the place. 'The colleges of Oxford approach more nearly to well-ordered cloisters of religious and monks than to an assembly of young men and youths congregated in their respective halls,' wrote one observer.[9] Another described the dress of the scholars as, 'almost the same as that of the Jesuits, their gowns reaching down to their ancles'.[10] Magdalene may well have been concerned about the morals of her eldest son, but if anywhere in England was going to dampen his youthful exuberance, Oxford was the place.

Walton, whose timing is ridiculously out, records that the family lived at Oxford for four years during which time:

> Having entered *Edward* into *Queens Colledge*, and provided him a fit *Tutor*, she commended him to his Care; yet she continued there with him, and still kept him in a moderate awe of her self: and so much under her own eye, as to see and converse with him daily; but she managed this power over him without any such rigid sourness, as might make her company a torment to her Child; but with such a sweetness and complyance with the recreations and pleasures of youth, as did incline him willingly to spend much of his time in the company of his dear and careful Mother...and continued with him in *Oxford* four years: in which time, her *great* and *harmless wit*, her *chearful gravity*, and her *obliging behaviour*, gain'd her an acquaintance and friendship with most of any eminent worth or learning, that were at that time in or near that University; and particularly with Mr. *John Donne*, who then came accidentally to that place...[11]

It is an intriguingly inaccurate passage. Given that virtually every fact in it is wrong—Edward was at University College, not Queen's, and the Herbert family only remained in Oxford for a year at the most—we might be inclined to doubt the 'accidental' meeting with John Donne. In later life, however, Magdalene was very close to Donne, and it is by no means inconceivable that their friendship began when they bumped into each other in Oxford.

'MANY FRIENDS IN GENERALL, ONE IN SPECIALL.'
Outlandish Proverbs No.281

John Donne

At the time John Donne was acting as secretary to the Lord
Keeper, Sir Thomas Egerton, whose stepson Francis Wolley was
an undergraduate of around Edward's age. Egerton, like Donne,
was an apostate and had actually taken part in persecuting a
number of Catholics, including Edmund Campion.[12] If John
Donne and Magdalene Herbert did meet, it can only have been
the briefest of acquaintances, for there is no record of any deepen-
ing of the relationship until 1607 by which time Magdalene and
her family had left Oxford far behind them.[13]

Even if they did not meet at Oxford, however, John Donne's
name would soon have been familiar to Magdalene Herbert, for
just before Christmas 1601 he secretly married Ann More. Ann's
father was Sir George More, the same George More who had
advised and acted on behalf of the family during the time of
Edward's wardship and with whom Edward corresponded. The
marriage meant the end of John's employment with Sir Thomas
Egerton, as well as a prison sentence.[14] Perhaps, on hearing of the
way in which this daring, scandalous young man had duped one
of her family's oldest and most trusted friends, Magdalene Herbert recalled the young man she met briefly passing through
Oxford. By this time the family would have been in London, so it
is possible that Magdalene was even more closely involved with
this incident.

As to the picture of sweetness and light that Walton draws of
Magdalene's relationship with her son, it is worth remarking that,
despite the time he spent listening to his mother, Edward never
completed his degree.

The Herbert family probably only remained in Oxford for two
years, until 1601. During this time, however, George's education
would have begun. Perhaps it was his early exposure to the
academic atmosphere of the university town that instilled in
Herbert the love of learning that was to take him to Cambridge
for so many years. Certainly he would have begun his education
in the city, with private schoolteachers and tutors being hired by
Magdalene. In his autobiography, Edward refers time and time

again to the learning in which the boys were raised. His mother knew the importance of learning and intelligence and wit.

Then, in April 1601, the family moved to London.

5

1601-1603

Charing Cross

THE CHICKEN IS THE COUNTRIES, BUT THE CITIE EATES IT.
Outlandish Proverb No.108

Charing Cross

According to Edward, the family arrived in London in February 1601, just before the Essex rebellion.[1]

London in 1601 was a lively, expanding, increasingly crowded city. Magdalene and her family took a house near Charing Cross, in the village of Charing on the extreme western edge of the city. What made this area popular was the expansion along the Strand of palaces and houses of the gentry. In the 1550s, St Martin's Fields had been just that–a field. A map of 1585 shows quarrying and brick-making in the area.

To imagine the development of London in the sixteenth and early seventeenth century, it is best to imagine two separate cities; London and Westminster. They were linked by the Thames and by the road which was to become the Strand. Between these cities lay the village of Charing. During the latter half of the sixteenth century, the road between these two centres was developed, so that the village became part first of London and then Westminster as the housing continued to stretch westwards. The Strand was lined with palaces, their gardens sloping down to the river, where hundreds of boatmen plied their trade between Westminster and London Bridge, the capital's sole bridge across the Thames.

Despite the fact that by 1601 some 250,000 people were living in the capital, Londoners were still acutely aware of the countryside.[2] St Giles, Paddington, Mary-le-bone, Islington and Bethnal Green were still villages, separated from the city by green fields and market gardens. No Londoner lived more than a quarter of an hour's walk from the countryside.[3] Hackney, Hampstead and Highgate were even further out in the country, and thick forest began in the countryside just beyond Kentish Town.[4]

London, however, was still growing. 'Soon,' James I was to remark ruefully, 'London will be all England.'[5] But London was not all England. For most Englishmen it remained a distant, almost exotic place. In exactly the same way as the aged Queen Elizabeth had never seen the north of her kingdom, most Englishmen never saw the capital. To the young George it must have seemed an overwhelming, bewildering place after the relative calm of Oxford, and events that took place shortly after their arrival must have shown how vastly different this place was to the seclusion of Montgomery, or the academic tranquillity of Oxford.

'TAKE HEED OF THE WRATH OF A MIGHTY MAN, AND THE
TUMULT OF THE PEOPLE'
Jacula Prudentum No.1141

Their Neighbourhood and Essex's Rebellion

Stow's survey of London, first published in 1598 and revised in 1603, gives us a superb picture of the city at the time of the Herbert's arrival.

From the western gate of the city at the Temple, progressing along the Strand would have brought us past Essex House–until lately the home of Elizabeth's erstwhile favourite the Earl of Essex, and before him her previous favourite, Robert Dudley, Earl of Leicester. The house was a home of high hopes, desperate gambles and terrible failure. Essex had been in disgrace from 1599 when he had returned from Ireland without Elizabeth's permission. He had promised to tame the rebellious Irish and he had failed. He returned home broken and thwarted, and rumoured to be plotting with the same Irish rebels he had gone to destroy. So for the first six months of 1600, Elizabeth had him imprisoned, eventually setting him free, though leaving him without any income or influence.

Around the time that the Herberts were settling in Charing Cross, Essex returned to Essex House–just five minutes walk from where they lived–and plotted a last desperate act. He

planned to revolt, not against the Queen, but against her powerful
ministers and advisers, especially against Sir Robert Cecil. All
Essex wanted was to return to the Queen's favour and once again
to wield power. One evening in February 1601 he marched against
London trusting that the Londoners, with whom he was popular,
would rise to his cause.

He was wrong. They did not rise for the simple reason that,
whatever the excuse, the English still abhorred rebellion. Not
even Mary's terrible reign had provoked them to such an act.
Thus, despite the popularity of his cause and the general
unpopularity of Elizabeth, the barriers at the city gate held firm.
Essex had no choice but to retreat along the Thames, back to
Essex House, where he surrendered to the government forces. He
was tried for high treason and executed in the Tower.

Their close proximity to the plot was not the Herberts' only
connection with the business, although the other link is equally
tenuous. One of his co-conspirators was Sir Charles Danvers, who
had served with Essex in Ireland. His job in the plot was to
overpower the guard at the door of the Presence Chamber in
Whitehall Palace, while the Earl of Essex sent others to guard the
Court and Water Gate. Danvers was found guilty and condemned
to death. On 18 March 1601 between 7 and 8 a.m., he was brought
to the same scaffold that had been used for Essex, and beheaded.
Years later, Magdalene Herbert was to marry his younger
brother.[6]

Such was the history of Essex House. Separated from it by the
Milford Stairs was Arundel House, bought by the second Earl of
Arundel after being forfeited by his Catholic father. Then the
Strand stairs, leading down to the river's edge, affording the
passer-by a view of the boatmen scuttling along the Thames, and
beyond them the south bank, where the tall, wooden 'O's of the
theatres could be seen in the distance.

Somerset House was next, granted to the Queen when she was
still a princess, but long since discarded by her majesty. After the
hospital of the Savoy, the chapel of which, according to Stow,
'serveth now as a Parish church to the Tenements thereof neare
adioyning',[7] the traveller came to Bedford House, the magnificent
town residence of the Russell family, who would soon begin
developing the Convent Garden just across the road into the
magnificent Covent Garden estate. The house stretched from the

hospital of Savoy, west to Ivie Bridge, where Essex's enemy, Sir Robert Cecil, 'hath lately raysed a large and stately house of brick and timber, as also leviled and paued the high way neare adioining, to the great beautifying of that street and commoditie of passengers'.[8]

By 1601, 'Ivie Bridge' had been taken down, but Ivy Lane still led down to the Thames and to Durham House, which lay to the south of Charing Cross. Although built for the Bishop of London, it had not had a clerical inhabitant for many years. In some ways it was a house of bad omens: the ill-fated Lady Jane Grey had lived there, then Walter Raleigh, with his retinue of more than forty servants.

After passing Durham House, the Strand widened out into a broad junction. In the middle of the road was the Charing Cross, the memorial to Queen Eleanor, placed there by King Edward in commemoration of his dead wife. To one side was an old hospital and priory, 'where a Fraternitie was founded in the 15. of Edward the 4., but now the same is supressed and turned into tenements'[9]

North from the Charing Cross, past the little medieval church of St Martin-in-the-Fields, ran St Martin's Lane, which joined the two villages of Charing and St Giles-in-the-Field. On the west side of the junction, occupying the site of the modern Trafalgar Square, were the Royal mews where the King's falcons were caged or 'mew'd'.

To the south the road ran past St James's park, annexed by Henry VIII and walled with brick. Along with 'divers fair houses', there was a tilt-yard and a cockpit. Opposite the park stood the royal palace of White Hall with its orchards, tennis courts and bowling alleys. Beyond White Hall stood an arched gate, beyond which the road led to Westminster.

'THE HOUSE IS A FINE HOUSE, WHEN GOOD FOLKE ARE WITHIN'
Outlandish Proverb No.952

Location of their house

According to Stow, Charing Cross was at this time filled with 'diuerse faire buildings, Hosteries, and houses for Gentlemen and men of honor'.[10] For a long time no-one has accurately identified the location of the Herberts' London house, but recent researches have revealed a likely location.

Amy Charles in her *Life* postulated that Magdalene's house must have been near a church. Daniel W. Doerksen discovered that the Herberts lived in the parish of St Martin-in-the-Fields, the parish church for the Charing Cross area.[11] The parish records show that Magdalene Herbert and her family were residents in the area and regular donors to the parish funds. Their residence and donations continued after Mrs Herbert's marriage. Indeed, St Martin's was considered her parish church until 1625, only two years before her death.

Such records do not give any location of their house, until we come to two donations, of 15 and 30 shillings, for the years 1626-7 and 1627-8 respectively. These have been donated by 'Lord Harbert' (i.e. Edward) under the heading 'Little Churchlane'.[12]

By this time, Magdalene Herbert had moved to Chelsea with her second husband, Sir John Danvers, and the Charing Cross house would have been given over to the use of Edward. As there are no records of Edward having purchased a London house in the intervening time, we can be fairly certain that the house in Little Churchlane was the same as that in which the Herberts had settled when they first arrived in London.

Where, then, was 'Little Churchlane'? Leading to the church, presumably, but neither John Norden's map of 1600 nor Hollar's map of 1658 give any street names for the streets immediately surrounding St Martin's-in-the-Fields.[13] However, maps of Whitehall in 1682 show that the basic layout of the streets remained the same and we know that this side of London was not affected by the great fire of 1666.

It is in a map of 1747 that we first find a 'Church Lane'. It runs from St Martin's Lane, along the north side of St Martin's church, parallel with the Strand for a little way, and then turns down to meet the Strand.[14] Although drawn 150 years later, the road layout is almost exactly that of the earlier maps. In all probability, then, 'Little Churchlane' has become 'Church Lane' in the intervening time.

So it is likely that the Herberts took up residence in their house in Little Churchlane, which ran between St Martin's Lane and the Strand, skirting the north side of St Martin's Church. It was to be their home for the next seventeen years.

'HE THAT HATH CHILDREN, ALL HIS MORSELS ARE NOT HIS
OWNE.'
Outlandish Proverb No.423

The Household and the Kitchen Booke

In contrast with Magdalene Herbert's residence at Oxford, we
know a great deal about her life in Little Churchlane, mainly
through the existence of a 'Kitchen Booke', kept by her steward
John Gorse. Through the book, which begins on 11 April 1601, we
know who made up the household, what their expenses were,
what guests came to dinner and a great deal more.

The *Kitchen Booke*, which has been examined in great detail by
Amy Charles, is a snapshot of the social life of a household in the
seventeenth century. John Gorse was allotted money every week,
usually in amounts of either two or four pounds.[15]

The book shows, among other things, that Magdalene enjoyed
a large household and a regular turnover of guests. Once the
family had settled into their new home they celebrated with a
'drincking' at which twenty-eight people joined the festivities, not
only 'drincking' but enjoying a meal of veal, lamb and eggs. The
next day was Easter Sunday and this time, twenty-nine people sat
down to meals. They were not necessarily the same guests – the
Kitchen Booke attests to the wide variety and diversity of Magdalene's friends in London.[16]

At the beginning of the book, Magdalene has written the
names of the 'regular' members of her household. Under the
headings of Gentlemen and Gentlewomen, there are all the members of her family, except William and Charles (who did not join
their mother until 29 April), her nephew Richard Newport, and
'Eliza: Detten', presumably a friend of the family. The gentlefolk
are augmented by ten servingmen, 'Jone Vaughan', a nurse, and
three 'chambermayds'.[17]

A house to accommodate some thirty people must have been a
large one, and we know from entries in the *Kitchen Booke* that the
house in Little Churchlane had gardens and grounds for keeping
pigs and poultry. Indeed, the largesse of Magdalene Herbert's
table incited a rather waspish comment from Edward who many
years later commented that Magdalene 'tooke house and kept a
greater Family then became either my Mother's widdows estate
or such young beginners as wee were.'[18]

Amy Charles goes into considerable detail about the guests attending the Herbert table, but only two deserve special mention, for they provide an example of a significant element in the Herbert household – the love of music. The *Kitchen Booke* records that both John Bull and William Byrd came for meals with the Herberts.[19] Both of the Doctors of Music were members of the Chapel Royal.

Along with visits from prominent composers and practitioners, the family also enjoyed professional performances and other services. The *Kitchen Booke* records fees paid for musicians, the visit of a wind-instrument maker and a couple of concerts by 'a Blynde harper and his boys'. This love of music was reflected throughout the household; George and Edward both played the lute, and Donne in his funeral sermon to Magdalene Herbert attested that the family ended each sabbath with 'a generall, with a cheerfull *singing of Psalmes*'.[20] Later in George's life, he would attend a weekly music group in Salisbury as well as setting his own poems to music.

'INFANTS MANNERS ARE MOULDED MORE BY THE EXAMPLE
OF PARENTS, THEN BY THE STARS AT THEIR NATIVITIES.'
Jacula Prudentum No.1060

Education of the Children

By this time, George Herbert was eight. Apart from the few clues given to us by the *Kitchen Booke*, we know little about him. However, we do know that his education, if it had not formally begun in Oxford, was now begun in earnest. A Mr Phillips was the main tutor, although he was generally accompanied by a deputy, probably the Mr Ireland who is mentioned once and with whom William and Charles spent the summer. George also spent the summer under the tuition of Will Heather (or Heyther) who lived near Westminster in a house he shared with the historian William Camden.[21]

From books purchased for George during this time, we know that he was working on his Latin (both Cato Senior and Cordelius were purchased along with a 'Coppie and Phrase booke'). Probably Magdalene Herbert herself took a major hand in the children's learning.

The Herberts turned out to be a well-educated, lively and
cultured family. Charles and George both excelled at university.
All the brothers seem to have had a natural facility for languages;
George's poetic gifts were, if not equalled, then at least echoed in
Edward and Henry; and to Edward we must also ascribe one of
the earliest major English works of philosophy. As Edward
recalled, all the children were 'brought up in learning' and certainly every effort was made to turn out cultured, rennaissance
men.[22] As for the daughters, they would most likely have been
educated at home. Mrs Herbert was a living testimony to the
advantages of education for women; she was not likely to neglect
advancing her daughters in that way.

'THE BEST BRED HAVE THE BEST PORTION.'
Outlandish Proverb No.953

Edward Herbert Comes of Age

There is a memorandum, drawn up by Magdalene Herbert,
which summarises the history of the relationship between her and
her son. Beginning 'The case betwene my sonne and me is this,' it
records the efforts that Magdalene put in on her son's behalf
following the death of her husband.

As well as adding some £400 of her own money to the estate,
she paid off her husband's debts. It cost her around £800 to
secure Edward's wardship and then a further £1,000 to arrange
Edward's marriage. This was seen as a good investment however,
as the marriage was thought to be worth £30,000.[23]

As we have seen, their hopes were to be cruelly dashed. As the
memorandum makes clear:

> [The] estate (contrary to our expectancy) beinge intangled
> with great debts, and vpon these extreme forfectures as the
> brech of one might have bye the ov[er]throwe of her whole
> estate, and neyther of them able neyther in yers or abilityes
> to vndertake the paym[t] of them, w[th] many griefs of minde
> and hazard of mine estate (if his wief had died before issue
> betwene them) I vndertook the paym[t] of them, repayinge
> myself as I could w[th] the receipt of her land, w[ch]
> notw[th]standing they came in by pieces, in comparison of

the greate summes wch I expended for the debts yet all layd
together equalled not my disbursem^ts by much, how much
I have payd more then I received I cannot justly say
because we differ vpon the accompt.

She goes on to claim that she has spent far more on Edward
and his wife than the £10 a year which the Court of Wards
stipulated: 'I have yerlye spent vpon him in his education and in
maytenance of his famelye...£500 for these 7 yeres whereby I
have not only bredd him in such sort as he now is, but also
[pre]vented his runninge in debt whiles he was vnder age...'

The document concludes with Mrs Herbert's 'demande' that
Edward give the sums intended by his father (£1,000 to each of his
sisters for dowries, and annuities of £40 to each of his brothers).
All she asks from Edward is 'your consideracons what you think
me worthy of'.[24]

The inspiration behind this document was the simple fact that
in 1603 Edward Herbert achieved his majority. He was twenty-
one. The document was intended to go before a committee to
draw up an abitration award. The committee confirmed the
£1,000 for the sisters, but fixed the brothers' annuities at £30. In
the ensuing years, the smallness of the sum was compounded by
the difficulty of persuading Edward to part with the cash. Getting
money out of Edward Herbert was an exhausting and often
fruitless task.

While it was not unusual to enshrine family affairs in legally
binding documents, it is curious to read the defence of a mother's
conduct with regard to her son. The document may well have
been intended merely as a legal safeguard, but it reads like the
words of one who feels she has been wronged. Magdalene justifies
her own, undoubtedly generous, behaviour with the fervour of a
litigant in a legal dispute. She is justifying her management of
Edward's affairs—and it is clear that she was the person who
managed his affairs, not his guardian Sir Francis Newport.

Edward, of course, remembered the episode slightly dif-
ferently:

My Mother though shee had all my Fathers Leases and
goods which were of greate Ualue yet shee desired mee to
vndertake that Burthen of providing for my brothers and
sisters which to gratify my Mother as well as those soe

neare me I was voluntarily content to provide thus farre as
to give my six brothers thirty pounds a piece yearely
during theire lives and my three sisters 1000 pounds a piece
which portions married them to those I haue
abouementioned.[25]

The succeeding years demonstrated how difficult it was to get
Edward to live up to these obligations that he had apparently been
so happy to shoulder. But the wording of the passage is telling;
his mother insists he undertake the 'burthen', despite 'having all
my Fathers leases and goods which were of greate value'. It is
clear that Magdalene's appeal to the legal process was the only
way in which she felt she could ensure just treatment for her other
children. For Edward's part, even writing years after the event,
he is still bitter that this well-off woman should have imposed this
unnecessary expense on him, in the very moment that he had at
last come into some form of financial security. The coolness
between Edward and his mother is only too apparent, a coolness
that succeeding years were to do nothing to thaw.

6

1603-1609

Westminster

1603

By early 1603 it was clear that the old Queen was dying.

She had ruled her country for forty-five years, having ascended to the throne at a time when England had been at its lowest ebb. She had brought stability and power to her realm, overseeing the re-establishment of the Protestant faith, and then defending this protestant country against all that her Catholic enemies could throw at it.

'Though I be a woman,' she told Parliament upon one occasion, 'I have as good a courage answerable to my place as ever my father had. I am your anointed Queen. I will never be by violence constrained to do anything. I thank God I am endued with such qualities that if I were turned out of the realm in my petticoat, I were able to live in any place in Christendom.'[1]

Nevertheless, age and the long war with Spain had taken its toll upon the resourceful and determined Queen. The French diplomat De Maisse recorded:

> As for her face, it is and appears to be very aged. It is long and thin, and her teeth are very yellow and unequal...Many of them are missing so that one cannot understand her easily when she speaks quickly...Her figure is fair and tall and graceful in whatever she does; so far as may be she keeps her dignity, yet humble and graciously withal.[2]

Her final years had not been the happiest of her reign. There had been the painful treachery of Essex. There had been the breakdown of peace talks with Spain. The economy in general—and the price of wheat in particular—was being attacked by inflation. Prices of all manner of goods were held artificially high by the system of monopolies which allowed a merchant to buy the monopoly of his goods from the crown. In the Parliament of 1601, when the list of monopolies was read out, an enraged member asked sarcastically, 'Is not bread there?'—such was the extent of this trade.[3] On her return from opening this, her final Parliament, few cheered her on her way.[4]

Nevertheless, she had steered a path through the political storm with her usual skill. She had learned in her sister's reign 'how to keep silent' and throughout her life she demonstrated better than anyone before or since the fine art of doing nothing. She did not marry and so no dangerous factions developed; she let the dispute between Puritan and Papist lie. Even in her old age, she refused to name a successor. Her policy was always to let such things take their course. Such fine political judgement was one of the main reasons her reign was so long: she never wasted her energies on what did not matter.

Now, however, that long reign was drawing to a close. A little while before her death, Edward Herbert had met the aging Queen:

> Curiosity, rather then Ambition brought mee to Court.
> And as it was the manner of those tymes for all men to
> kneele downe before the greate Queene Elizabeth, who
> then raigned, I was likewise vpon my knees in the Presence
> Chamber when shee passed by to the Chappell in
> whitehall. As soone as shee sawe mee shee stopt and
> swearing her usual Oath demaunded who is this?

The Queen's 'usual Oath' was the exclamation, 'God's Death!'. In answer to her question, it was explained to her that the handsome young man was Edward Herbert, married to the daughter of Sir William Herbert.

> The Queene herevpon looked attentively vpon mee and
> swearing againe her Ordinary oath said, It is pitty he was
> married soe young and thereupon gave mee her hand to

kisse twice, both tymes gently Clapping mee on the
Cheeke.[5]

She may have been old, but she could still recognise a handsome face when she saw one and she had lost none of her ability to
wind young men around her little finger. Indeed, handling such
audiences had always been one of her great skills. When an
audience was granted, according to Sir John Hayward, 'her eye
was set upon one, her ear listened to another, her judgement ran
upon a third, to a fourth she addressed her speech; her spirit
seemed to be everywhere and yet so entire in her self, as it seemed
to be nowhere else'.[6]

She died on 24 March 1603, to be succeeded by James Stuart,
James VI of Scotland. When James ascended the throne, Elizabeth's popularity was at its lowest point. Perhaps one of James'
most remarkable achievements is that he made her already hard-
pressed people view her reign with affection.

'HEE THAT IS IN A TOWNE IN MAY LOSETH HIS SPRING.'
Outlandish Proverbs No.988

James I and the Plague

Elizabeth's cousin, James was thirty-seven years old at the time of
his accession. Resolutely Protestant, he was full of nervous
energy, and presented to his new subjects a strange mixture of
acute intelligence and base vulgarity. Even in an age of minimal
hygiene standards, James' personal habits were not the cleanest,
and to cap it all, he had a slight physical impediment: his tongue
was too large for his mouth and he tended to slobber into his
drink. Almost his first act on entering the country was to ask the
Privy Council for money. It did not bode well.[7]

Edward Herbert, fortified by the success of his reception by
the previous monarch, travelled to Stamford to meet the new
King at Burghley House.[8] He would have found the King surrounded by a large retinue of well-wishers, courtiers and hangers-
on all bound on the same mission; securing preferment. By 7
May, the crowds had increased still further as the King arrived on
the outskirts of London. The area was thronged with such 'multi-
tudes of people in high ways, fields, meadows, and on

trees... that they covered the beauty of the fields; and so greedy were they to behold the countenance of the King that, with much unruliness, they injured one another.'[9]

For some weeks, in anticipation of the new monarch's arrival, London had been packed to bursting. Visitors came either to see the new King, or to obtain preferment and employment. The sheer amount of visitors brought a much needed influx of money into the capital. In the words of Thomas Dekker, 'Trades that lay dead and rotten, and were in all men's opinion utterly damnbd, started out of their trance'.[10] The Herberts, aware of all the hustle and bustle around them, must have excitedly prepared to view King's triumphal procession.

Their hopes were to be dashed. On 11 May, James made his solemn entry to the Tower of London, but without passing through the city. He stayed for three days and then fled to Greenwich, for the new commercial life that had sprung up in the capital was a cruel deception: instead of economic recovery, London was struck by the plague.

It was by no means the first time that the cramped streets and narrow lanes of the city had played host to the pestilence, for the city was an ideal breeding ground for disease. Dirt and human refuse were generally thrown out onto the muddy highways. Dunghills blocked the narrow thoroughfares, barbers and surgeons would casually throw the results of their blood-letting out into the streets. Guts, entrails and also the water in which they had been boiled were likewise discarded by the butchers and tripe-wives of the city. The sheer amount of refuse on the streets meant that kites and crows were the most common birds to be seen.[11]

What made the plague of 1603 so horrendous was the sheer number of people in London at the time. Like a modern capital playing host to the Olympics, the city was crammed to bursting point with visitors. Thus when the disaster struck, it spread rapidly throughout the city. Once it had taken hold, of course, the visitors fled, along with everyone else capable of escaping. Commerce, cruelly tricked, died again, and the city was eerily empty. So complete was the desertion that grass was recorded as growing in Cheapside, one of the busiest thoroughfares of the city.

For those forced to remain, the situation was almost hopeless.

Most of the medical profession had fled, so there was no chance of getting treatment. As for the other cure, the cure of souls, few vicars stayed in their parishes to relieve their suffering flock. Among the notable exceptions was James Bamford, who stayed in his parish of St Olave's–where the plague struck more heavily than anywhere else–preaching and comforting the bereaved. Another exception was the Catholic priest Dom Joanne Marrino (known more prosaically as 'Roberts') who was, 'almost indefatigable in visiting the sick. His courage and loyalty was to be rewarded eight years later by being burned at the stake'.[12]

It is not known where the Herbert family went to escape this visitation. In later visitations they escaped to Chelsea. Certainly at least one of George's elder brothers was well away from it, for records show that the ten-year-old Charles Herbert had by this time entered Winchester school.

Wherever they fled, if they had anticipated seeing the festivities surrounding a coronation they were to be disappointed. James was unable to make his triumphal pilgrimage through the city's streets. He stayed at Windsor for most of June. On 25 July, he and his retinue travelled along the Thames to Westminster where his coronation took place. It must have been a strangely empty affair, for hardly any Londoners were there. Access to Westminster had been barred both by road and by river. The planned pageants and 'Triumphant Passage' were postponed until winter. Immediately after the coronation James returned to the relative safety of Hampton Court.[13] It was not until winter that the plague began to lessen. In the six months that it had really taken hold, the plague of 1603 had carried off more than 30,000 victims.

'THEY FAVOUR LEARNING WHOSE ACTIONS ARE WORTHY OF A LEARNED PEN.'
Jacula Prudentum No.1061

Lancelot Andrewes and Westminster School

The next year, George's sister Elizabeth was married to Henry Johnes of Albemarles, probably at Wroxeter.[14] The bond between George and his eldest sister was always close; later in life she would give him much-needed money for books and he would ride many miles to attend to her in the long, lingering sickness that led eventually to her death.

Unlike his elder brother Charles, George did not go to Winchester school, but to the much nearer establishment at Westminster. He first started there as a day scholar, probably in 1604. Westminster School had been refounded in 1561 by Queen Elizabeth herself. It stood to the south side of the Abbey Church, near some fields, and on the edge of the city itself. In all probability, Herbert was admitted whilst the establishment was under the charge of the great Protestant divine, Lancelot Andrewes.[15]

Andrewes had become Dean of Westminster in 1601. An immensely gifted and articulate clergyman, he had been a favourite of Elizabeth (it was Andrewes who preached the funeral sermon when she was buried in Westminster Abbey). James, too, was to come to rely on Andrewes and when the work began on the new translation of the Bible, Andrewes was the man entrusted with the general editorship. As Dean of Westminster he had responsibility for Westminster School. Although he was not officially required to teach, he often took classes and he would meet the boys at mealtimes and oversee the tuition and general running of the school. As an eminent scholar of Greek and Hebrew, it is hardly surprising that the curriculum majored heavily in classical languages, and Andrewes encouraged the boys 'unfolding to them the best Rudiments of the Greek Tongue, and the Elements of the Hebrew Grammar'.[16]

He would have found a ready pupil in the young George, who, on arrival at the school had already been taught the rudiments of several languages. No doubt his faculty for languages was already evident. Andrewes, as well, took more than just a general interest in the boys. They would often accompany him on walks to the school's house at Chiswick: 'he never walked to Chiswick for his recreation without a brace of this young Fry, and in that wayfaring liesure, had a singular dexterity to fill those narrow vessels with a funnel.'[17] However, despite the best efforts of later biographers to maintain links between the great clergyman and the young poet, George could only have come under the Dean's influence for a short period of time. In 1605 Andrewes left Westminster to become Bishop of Chichester. In later life, George would even write in direct opposition to Andrewes' preaching style, which James I once described as '[playing] with his Text, as a Jack-an-apes does, who takes up a thing and tosses and playes with it, and then he takes up another, and playes a little with it'.[18]

At the time of George's entry, Westminster School was made up of some 120 pupils, consisting of the King's Scholars, the pensioners; peregrines and oppidans; and the choristers. All were under the rule of the headmaster, Richard Ireland, who was in charge of the school from 1599 to 1610.[19] The pensioners boarded either with the Dean, or with the cathedral prebendaries or masters. The peregrines were county boys who boarded with relatives or friends nearby. George would have been an oppidan – a son of a resident in or near Westminster.

The elite of the school were the King's Scholars, who were chosen – or 'elected' – from boys with at least a year's standing in the school. The election was unique at the time in that it was composed, at least partially, by a competitive examination. George's education at home stood him in good stead and, in 1605 at the age of twelve, he was 'elected' as a King's Scholar, thus moving from being a day-visitor to becoming a boarder.[20]

The curriculum centred around the classical disciplines of grammar (hence 'grammar' schools), rhetoric and logic, taught mainly through Latin texts. At Westminster, however, there were two other aspects which no doubt affected George's life. One was the study of Greek, in which he was to become highly proficient. The other was the study of music. The prominence of music on the curriculum was due largely to the proximity of the Abbey church and also by the attendance at school of the Westminster Abbey choristers. Although most of their day was spent in the Abbey itself, they attended the school for two hours each weekday.

Like that of most schoolboys of the time, George's life at Westminster was harsh. The regime centred around various forms of religious ritual. The boys were woken at 5 a.m. by the dormitory monitors and moved at once into their devotions. They would begin each day with a service which included Latin prayers, the general confession, the Lord's Prayer (twice), a hymn, three psalms, a lesson from Proverbs, the *Te Deum*, another lesson – this time from the Sermon on the Mount – the Apostles' Creed, several collects and a prayer for the King.[21] After this rude awakening, they would make their beds, sweep the floor and go to the cloisters to wash. At 6 a.m. the day scholars would arrive and the entire school, led by the second master, would engage in further devotions.

Work began at 7. At 8 a.m. the headmaster would arrive, and would set a Latin exercise. Dinner was taken in the Great Hall at 10 or 11 o'clock (preceded, of course, by prayers and thanksgivings for the royal family and a grace). At this meal, the Dean and other Abbey dignitaries would join the scholars, sitting at their high table at the end of the hall. Some boys would be chosen to read the Scriptures or a Latin text. Others would be sent a morsel of the better food from the high table, with a theme on which the favoured recipient would have to extemporise an epigram. The meal ended with—surprise, surprise—a long grace.[22]

Work continued through the afternoon until supper at 6 o'clock, accompanied, like dinner, by a full complement of graces and prayers. An hour's break was allowed, but then it was back to work at 7 o'clock. After evening prayers in the dormitory, the King's Scholars went to bed.

Sundays were, comparatively speaking, days of rest. The boys attended services in the Abbey, taking notes on the sermons. Once a week a half-holiday was allowed, and the boys also celebrated the usual complement of Saint's Days and Holidays. Physical punishment was common—indeed, birching was accepted as the standard method of helping boys remember their studies.[23]

Such was George's life from 1605, when he was elected as a King's Scholar, to 1609 when he went to Trinity College, Cambridge. The effect of such a harsh regime on a boy of delicate health can readily be imagined. Nevertheless intellectually at least, it set the foundation for George's life. His mastery of Latin and Greek was to bloom during his years at university; his love of music was to stay with him throughout his life; and the mass exposure to religious services and private prayer, added to the piety of his mother, left him with a deep and personal faith. If he was never a disciple of Dean Andrewes to the degree that many would claim, he always had a high regard for the services and ritual of the Established Church. To a large extent, this was a legacy of his years at Westminster.

7

1609

Charing Cross, London

'SINCE YOU KNOW ALL, AND I NOTHING, TELL ME WHAT I
DREAMED LAST NIGHT.'
Outlandish Proverbs No.336

Gunpowder Plot

> In the third yeare of King James The Gunpowder Treason
> hapening My selfe who was chosen Knight of the shire for
> Merionethshire...did then lodg in my Mothers house
> neare Charing Crosse. The night before this horible
> Conspiracy was to bee acted I was two seuerall tymes
> warned in my sleepe not to goe to the Parliament that day
> which though I tooke but for dreaming fell out to bee an
> Admonition.[1]

Were he not warned by his premonition, Edward would have
made his way to Parliament that day in November 1605, where he
was serving at the time. As it was, Sir Walter Cope called on him
early the next morning and told him about the audacious plot to
blow up the King in Parliament. Edward was advised not to leave
the house until matters were a little more settled. In the end, he
took a company of men to Dudley in Staffordshire to catch the
remaining rebels. In a manner rather typical of many of Edward's
exploits, things did not quite work out as planned. The conspirators had already been rounded up by the time they got there and
in a farcical misunderstanding, the leader of the company, Sir
Thomas Dutton, was mistaken for one of the conspirators by the
local militia and almost thrown into the fire.[2]

What shocked people even more than the actual intention of
killing the King was the very suddenness of the intended death.

Everybody, it was felt, had a right to prepare themselves for death. Soldiers preparing to fight, traitors on the scaffold, plague victims in the gutter; they all had the opportunity to repent and to call upon God. What shocked men like Lancelot Andrewes (who had been consecrated bishop two days earlier and was due to have been in the House that day to take his place in the House of Lords) was that such an attempt offered its intended victims no chance to 'pull the brand from the burning'.[3] The shock news of the plot and the general sense of relief that it had failed must have buzzed among the schoolboys at Westminster, who lived only a few hundred yards from the scene of the attack.

Parliament was not Edward's only concern during this period. When not involved in London, he was spending most of his time at the family castle at Montgomery, which he was gradually rebuilding. There were still many tensions between Edward and his mother. She wrote to their old friend Sir George More on 14 March 1607:

> Since Wednesday, Ned Herbert is rod home towards his wife, he hath put me in no less, but another feare, since the ending of that you know of, which makes me know the miseries of this lyfe, and to place my contentment in that, I hope and looke for, and in nothing I have or inioy.[4]

Like many mothers before and since, her eldest son had driven Magdalene to the comforts of religion. Edward's brother Charles was also being 'troblesom' to both correspondent and recipient, although (as with Edward) exactly how, we are left to guess.

At least another of her family was now out of her hands. A little less than a year after the gunpowder plot, her daughter Margaret was married to John Vaughan in the church of St Nicholas, Montgomery, 'by which match', wrote Edward, 'some former differences betwixt our house and that were appeased and reconciled'.[5] The differences between him and his mother were not so easily mended.

'THE BEST MIRROUR IS AN OLD FRIEND.'
Outlandish Proverbs No.296

Magdalene Herbert and John Donne

It was in 1607 that Magdalene either began (or if Walton is correct, renewed) a friendship that was to last for the rest of her life. Since his marriage to Ann More, John Donne had been living in poverty in the village of Mitcham, adding a child to his family almost every year. He had no regular employment, and he and his wife were exiled from the society of her family.[6] Faced with such a situation and attempting to escape the claustrophobia of his tiny Mitcham cottage, Donne would make regular forays to London. He even took lodgings off the Strand, not far from the Herbert home in Charing Cross. To be fair, it was not only that he wanted to socialise and to escape the domestic pressures; he was trying to find employment, which meant being in the right place at the right time. In 1605-6, he went abroad as companion to Sir Walter Chute, but in 1607 he was back in London.[7]

Perhaps it was during one of his periods in London that Donne met Edward Herbert, and through Edward, Magdalene. Or it is possible that on the basis of their previous acquaintance, he approached her to ask her to mediate between him and his father-in-law, Sir George More, with whom, as we have seen, Magdalene was in regular contact.

Whatever the case, a warm friendship seems to have sprung up between the two. She was, according to Walton, to prove 'one of his most bountiful Benefactors'.[8] Four letters from Donne to Magdalene Herbert survive, all written during the summer of 1607. It was Magdalene to whom Donne sent his first religious poems—the La Corona sequence—along with a poem dedicating the set to her.[9]

To Magdalene too, Donne dedicated a poem celebrating a woman in middle age, 'The Autumnall':

> No *Spring*, nor *Summer* Beauty hath such grace,
>   As I have seen in one *Autumnall* face.
> Young Beauties force our love, and that's a Rape,
>   This doth but *counsaile*, yet you cannot scape.[10]

Only a relationship of trust could have survived the opening lines which, as John Carey says, 'teeter on the brink of insult'.[11] But insofar as it is insulting, it is the kind of insult that friends enjoy together. It reads more like an 'in-joke'.

It is clear that they enjoyed an easy, relaxed relationship. After all, the poem is about getting old. It talks of a woman nearing fifty years of age; it jokes of tombs and going 'downe the hill'. It is the kind of affectionate joking held between two people of middle age (Donne was past forty at this time) who jest together about being 'past it'. But Magdalene is evening, not night, autumn, not winter, and the comparison between her and older women is cruelly and mockingly made in caricaturing those:

> *Winter-faces*, whose skin's slacke;
>   Lanke, as an unthrift's purse, but a soules sacke;
> Whose Eyes seeke light within, for all here's shade;
>   Whose mouths are holes, rather worne out, then made;
> Whose every tooth to a severall place is gone,
>   To vexe their soules at Resurrection;
> Name not these living Deaths-heads unto mee,
>   For these not *Ancient*, but *Antique* bee.[12]

After the savagery of this attack, the poem draws back to the gentle, elegaic coolness and quietness of love in the 'evening'. It is a poem full of 'affection', rather than passion. It is a moderate, a 'seasonable' love. Of course, it is a love poem—which is not the same thing as saying that Donne was in love with her. Donne's poetic imagination has simply used their friendship as a launching point. Nevertheless, there is at the heart of the poem the true sense of their relationship—gentle, affectionate, calm, and humorous.

'GOSSIPS ARE FROGS, THEY DRINKE AND TALKE'
Outlandish Proverbs No.275

Remarriage

Magdalene must have been a confident, self-assured woman for Donne to address her so. She was certainly still attractive—one could never write such a poem to someone who was not. Indeed, it was this beauty, self-confidence and intelligence that led to the next major development in the life of the Herbert family. For, on 26 February 1609, she married Sir John Danvers.

It was an unlikely match. Born in 1588, John Danvers was only twenty-one at the time. The biographer John Aubrey records, with his usual cattiness, 'she was old enough to have been his Mother' and goes on to say, 'He maried her for love of her Witt. The Earl of Danby [Sir John's brother] was greatly displeased with him for this disagreable match.'[13]

Danvers was a well-known figure around town, a figure who in a later era would have been known as a 'beau'. 'He had', records Aubrey, 'in a faire Body an harmonicall Mind: In his Youth his Complexion was so exceedingly beautifull and fine that Thomas Bond Esqr. (who was his Companion in his Travells) did say, that the People would come after him in the Street to admire Him.'[14]

From the first, their marriage caused tongues to wag. When Donne first heard about it, he sent her a verse epistle ('To Mrs M. H.') in which he asks the paper he is writing on to reveal the identity of her husband–an identity he probably already knew. Donne was after contacts and must have figured that Sir John Danvers would be an extremely useful patron. Even so, the disparity in ages must have surprised even the romantic Donne. He was still making reference to the difference at her funeral service eighteen years later:

> For as the well tuning of an *Instrument*, makes *higher* and *lower* strings of one sound, so the inequality of their yeeres was thus reducit to an evennesse, that shee had a *cheerfulnesse* agreeable to his *youth*, and he a *sober staidnesse*, comformable to her *more yeares*. So that, I would not consider her, at so much more then *forty*, nor him, at so much lesse then *thirty*, at that time, but as their *persons* were made *one*, and their *fortunes* made one, by *mariage*, so I would put their yeeres into *one number* and finding a *sixty* betweene them, thinke them *thirty* a peece; for as twins of one houre, they liv'd.[15]

Donne was being generous. At the time of her marriage, she was probably nearer fifty than forty, and Danvers was only twenty-one. A graduate of Brasenose college, Oxford, he had been knighted by King James only a few months before their marriage, at Royston on 3 March 1608.[16]

It was not only the difference in ages that caused tongues to wag about Sir John Danvers. There were other rumours—that he was profligate, that he was unable to live within his means.

The Danvers had always been a talked-about family. John's older brothers Charles and Henry had spent some years in exile in France for killing a neighbour, Henry Long, in 1593 (their mother always claimed it was self-defence). Pardoned in 1598 the brothers returned, but as we have seen Charles was later tried and executed for his role in the Essex plot. The lands had been forfeited to the Crown, but the accession of James I saw the Danvers family return to favour. John's elder brother Henry was made Baron Danvers by James I. Among his many accomplishments, he was to found the 'physick garden' at Oxford.[17]

In many ways, John shared this strange mixture of culture and wrong-headedness. He certainly shared Henry's interest in gardening and was later to create magnificent Italianate gardens at Chelsea and Dauntsey. He had travelled abroad and, according to Aubrey, 'made good observations'.[18] He was a cultured and intelligent man, so much so that Bacon sent him the manuscript of his *History of Henry VII* for his comments before publication:

> Qd. Sir John, Your Lordship knowes that I am no Scholar. 'Tis no matter, said my Lord [Bacon]: I knowe what a Schollar can say; I would know what you can say. Sir John read it, and gave his opinion what he misliked...which my Lord acknowledged to be true, and mended it; Why, said he, a Scholar would never have told me this.[19]

That the match displeased his brother is hardly surprising, but it was a match typical of this flamboyant, passionate family.

No doubt the marriage with the comparatively well-off Magdalene helped his financial problems. For her part it certainly increased her social standing; she was now sister-in-law to Baron Danvers of Dauntsey, who had a close friendship with the Prince of Wales.

Amidst all the rumours and scandal, however, one can easily lose out on one simple fact: they were in love. John, after all, was a most eligible young man. He could have had his pick of well-dowried young ladies.

Instead he chose Magdalene. Undoubtedly her 'wit', as Aubrey says, attracted him. She was an acutely intelligent woman. Her looks, though fading, would still have been alluring. Perhaps also, he felt secure with her. Perhaps this spendthrift young man found someone who could manage him, who could guide and advise him, look after him. For all the years he lived with her—first at Charing Cross, and then at Chelsea—he was prosperous and, relatively speaking, successful. After her death and without her calming and managing influence, things were very different and his later years were to be spent struggling bitterly against debt, disappointment and disgrace.

That, however, was many years ahead. It is not known how they came to meet. Magdalene with her penchant for entertaining, possibly invited the young man to her house. Perhaps he came with John Donne, perhaps he had met Edward Herbert at court. Either way, George and the rest of his brothers and sisters now found themselves with a father for the first time in thirteen years. What is more, their new 'father' was only a few years older than George, and was actually younger than Edward. It does not seem to have adversely affected George. From the letters between them that have come down to us, it appears they enjoyed an easy relationship, more like that of two brothers than father and son.

8

1609-1618

Trinity College, Cambridge

'KNOWLEDGE IS NO BURTHEN'
Outlandish Proverbs No.692

University – 1609

The remarriage of George's mother took place during his last year at Westminster School. He had been an outstanding scholar whose talent had been noted by his teachers. Thomas Plume, writing a biographical note about Herbert's school-fellow, John Hacket, records the esteem in which both schoolboys were held:

> To tell how well [Hacket] passed the Circuit of that School, I need say no more but what his *Master Ireland* [the Headmaster] said, at parting, to *him* and *George Herbert*, who went from thence to *Trinity Colledge* in *Cambridge* by election together, That he expected to have credit by *them two* at the *University*, or would never hope for it afterwards by any while he lived: and added withal, that he need give them no counsel to follow their Books, but rather to study moderately, and use exercise; their parts being so good, that if they were careful not to impair their health with too much study, they would not fail to arrive to the top of learning in any *Art* or *Science*.[1]

George's brothers William and Charles had already progressed to university. William matriculated at Oxford, at Queen's College on 1 July 1608. Charles had left Winchester for New College, Oxford.[2] In 1609, after five years at Westminster School, it was George's turn to follow their example.

Westminster had a right to send three boys to Trinity College in Cambridge. In fact, the College was awash with old West-minsters–between 1600 and 1700 nearly half the Fellows of Trin-ity came from Westminster School.[3] Herbert, along with John Hacket and another boy–the rather exotically named Wal-singham Shirley–were duly named the Westminster Scholars at Trinity College, Cambridge for their year. They were admitted to the College on 5 May 1609.[4] It is likely that George actually began living in the university in autumn 1609, when he is first men-tioned in the Bursar's book as receiving two payments of three shillings and four pence each–the quarterly amount payable to students.[5]

It is at Cambridge that George Herbert suddenly comes alive for the modern biographer. Before 1609, we know a lot about him–where he lived, where he went to school, what kinds of things he learned, what events took place around him, even what his family ate–but we don't know him. There are little or no personal reminiscences of the young George. He is a shadowy, unsubstantial figure, one of a multitude of Jacobean schoolboys, living in the hubbub of London.

At Cambridge, however, Herbert emerges from the mists. University provided an environment in which he was to blossom and thrive. At Cambridge he took his first official posts, made orations in front of Royalty, and wrote letters home. Already an accomplished scholar, university gave him not only a chance to display his scholarship but also to mingle with some of the finest brains and most influential people of his age. It was at Cambridge, too, that George Herbert first put his mind to the serious business of seeking preferment. Most important, it is at Cambridge that he wrote his first poetry.

Cambridge was a far cry from crowded, teeming London and the rigorous regime of Westminster. First and foremost, it had a totally different religious atmosphere. Cambridge had long been the home of Protestantism, even at times of Puritanism. In its early days, the university had a reputation as a hotbed of Lollar-dry (in the same way as it was to have a reputation for Commu-nism in the 1930s)[6]. Though such extremes of radical thought had long since been suppressed, the university still gloried in its key role in the English Reformation. Erasmus had been Lady Mar-garet Professor of Divinity from 1511 to 1513; at the White Horse Inn, the Cambridge Reformers had met in secret to discuss the works of the German Reformers such as Luther; the architects of English Protestantism were almost exclusively Cambridge men; twelve out of the thirteen compilers of the English Prayer Book had been educated at Cambridge. Cranmer, Latimer and Ridley, though martyred at Oxford, were all products of Cambridge and had taught at Cambridge for many years. Calvinism had spread rapidly through the university in the 1560s and 1570s.[7] The religious atmosphere that Herbert entered was therefore, radically different from the High Anglican curriculum of Westminster.

'A DILIGENT SCHOLLER, AND THE MASTER'S PAID.'
Outlandish Proverbs No.183

University Life

George was sixteen when he entered university. It was by no means unusual for undergraduates to be so young. The Earl of Essex entered at eleven, Francis Bacon at thirteen, and Milton was to enter at seventeen.[8] Among his older brothers, who had preceded him to university, Edward had been fourteen and Charles sixteen. William, who matriculated at Oxford from Queens College in 1608, was unusually old at nineteen.[9]

The comparative youth of the undergraduates was the reason for the frequent use of corporal punishment at both Oxford and Cambridge. Until attaining their degree, students were still *non-adulti*. They were therefore liable to suffer the birch for any form of ill-discipline. Other punishments included fines, impositions or, ultimately, expulsion from the university. Crimes which the university habitually punished included drunkenness, 'the taking of tobacco', brawling in public, and–especially–swimming or bathing in any of the local rivers.[10]

Trinity College was at this time the most notable college in the university. Its members probably numbered more than 400, the largest number at any Cambridge college. The Master at the time of Herbert's admission was Dr Thomas Neville, who had been appointed by Queen Elizabeth herself. From the start, he determined to make Trinity the largest and most powerful college in the university. Aided by the architect Ralph Symons, he engaged on an ambitious scheme of building: erecting the great hall and

kitchen, building the Queen's Gate and completing the Great
Court (which meant moving the huge Edward III gate, stone by
stone, and resiting it to the north). In the middle of the Great
Court, he placed a magnificent fountain, which, in George's time
would have been painted.[11] To the west of the college, between
the hall and the river he added another court now known as
Neville's Court.[12]

Trinity College still had a strongly Puritan element in it,
despite the best efforts of the authorities to drive such elements
out. It was second only to Emmanuel for the number of young
men it sent to New England.[13] Some years after Herbert's period
at the college, it was reported that 'in some tutors' chambers the
private prayers are longer and louder by far at night than they are
at Chapel in the evening'. Even so, Trinity instilled in Herbert a
tolerance for a wide range of customs and practices. Throughout
his life he hated schisms and religious bigotry. Some of this
feeling, at least, must have come from Trinity, where at Chapel
'they lean, or sit or kneel at prayers, every one in a several posture
as he pleases. At the name of Jesus, few will bow, and when the
creed is repeated, many of the boyes, by some men's directions,
turn towards the west door.'[14]

Cambridge, like Oxford, operated on the tutorial system. In a
way, this was similar to the present system, except that far fewer
pupils were the tutor's responsibility and the relationship
between tutor and student was far more intimate. This was
mainly due to the age of the pupils. A tutor was *in loco parentis*.[15]
Often the tutor would be only of BA standing, perhaps only a few
years older than the students under his care. He would be
appointed to two or three pupils by arrangement with the students or their parents, or occasionally by order of the Master.[16]

It is not known who George's tutor was, but whoever it was,
their relationship would have been quite intimate. The intimacy
of this relationship can be seen from the fact that the tutor usually
lived with his pupils. They would share a fairly large room. Small
partitions formed 'studies' by each window, each furnished with a
chair, a desk and some storage for books. Meals were served in
the centre of the room. The students slept on low beds which
were stored during the day under the tutor's bed.[17]

Hacket's Tutor was 'Dr. *Simson*, who wrote the *Church History*'. Among the other lecturers were; 'Dr. *Cumber* a great Crit-

ick, Dr *Richardson Regius Professor*, Dr. *Nevil* a very splendid
and sumptuous Governor; the great Hebrician and Chronologer
Mr. *Lively*, one of the *Translators* of the *Bible*, the famous and
memorable Dr. *Whitgift*, sometime Master, afterwards Archbishop of *Canterbury*'.[18]

It was extremely rare for students to live in private lodgings,
and with everyone living in college the problem of overcrowding
was acute. For recreation there were no organised games, but
there was the college tennis court (built by Neville at the enor-
mous cost of £120), or archery. There was also rough football,
which was little more than a free fight between Trinity and St
John's. It is hard to imagine Herbert ever played an active part in
such games.

The curriculum followed the traditional pattern with which
Herbert would already have been familiar. Rhetoric, logic and
theology formed the basis of the studies, but the BA degree
included a large amount of general study. It was only when a
student had qualified as Bachelor of Arts that he proceeded to
more specialised study.[19]

'LOVE ASKES FAITH, AND FAITH FIRMENESSE.'
Outlandish Proverbs No.544

Poetic Aims

The only problem with studying at Cambridge was health.
Throughout his life George had a fragile constitution and the
damp fen country caused him considerable ill-health. The
crowded university conditions also meant that plague was often a
problem. At least three epidemics occurred during Herbert's
undergraduate years – in 1608, 1610 and 1611. In the last of these,
429 persons died in the town.[20] The surrounding fens only added
to the marshy and damp climate of the city. Throughout his years
at Cambridge, Herbert was often to travel away from the city,
literally to get a breath of 'fresh air'. Indeed, his first few months
at the University appear to have been troubled by ill-health. In
early 1610 he wrote to his mother, 'But I fear that the heat of my
late *Ague* hath dryed up those springs, by which Scholars say, the
Muses use to take up their habitations.'[21]

The letter, of which the only extract we have is in Walton's

Life, accompanied a poem that he sent to his mother. From his early years poetry must have figured largely in the life of the Herberts. George was not the only poet in his family, by any means. We have a considerable body of work by Edward, as well as occasional verse by Henry, satires by Thomas and even four lines of Latin verse from Charles. Of poets outside the family, he would have known the work of Donne only too well, not only through verses received by his mother but also through verses exchanged with Edward. Possibly he saw work by others of Edward's circle, including Aurelian Townsend, Thomas Carew and Ben Jonson.[22]

Nevertheless, George did not want to write the kind of love verses and Donne-imitations favoured by his brother. In the letter he declares his aim:

> To reprove the vanity of those many Love-poems, that are daily writ and consecrated to *Venus*; nor to bewail that so few are writ, that look towards *God* and *Heaven* . . . my meaning (*dear Mother*) is in these Sonnets, to declare my resolution to be, that my poor Abilities in *Poetry* shall be all, and ever consecrated to God's glory.[23]

The young student is taking himself very seriously in this letter. Given his mother's religious piety it may be that he is writing to reassure her that he is not slipping away from the faith, that he is 'looking after himself'. There is, likewise, an air of youthful enthusiasm about the two sonnets. Perhaps his new surroundings had fired his imagination, but even if the decision to reject 'these many Love-poems' was crystallised by the serious, protestant atmosphere of Trinity, his resolve to use his gifts to God's glory was a conviction that guided George's poetic talents throughout his life.

This letter and the accompanying poem are significant because they are the first indication of such a conviction:

> Why are not *Sonnets* made of thee? and layes
>   Upon thine Altar burnt? Cannot thy love
>   Heighten a spirit to sound out thy praise
> As well as any she?[24]

One must not, however see a calling as a sacrifice. Like any poet,

Herbert was writing about that which inspired and excited him. He rejected love-poetry, but there is no evidence that it ever held any great lure for him anyway. By choosing to write divine poetry Herbert was not pushing away a deep desire to write romantic verse, and the assertion by a Victorian critic that the 'early poetry of Herbert, courtly and amatory; was all destroyed...about 1627' is mere make-believe.[25] What burned within George, what made him want to write poetry at all, was simply God.

Although there were times when he strayed, when he used his poetry to seek preferment or to pay compliments, he remained true to his poetic vocation. Throughout his life he used his poetic gifts to praise God, even when he felt he had little to praise God for. The heart of George Herbert's poetry – poetry which he began writing during his Cambridge years – is that it was part of a living relationship with God. When this relationship was damaged, then so was his poetry: 'When my devotions could not pierce/ Thy silent eares;/ Then was my heart broken, as was my verse.'[26] And when God's love has renewed his 'shrivel'd heart', then once again he can 'live and write...And relish versing'.[27]

'AMONGST GOOD MEN TWO MEN SUFFICE.'
Outlandish Proverbs No.885

Friends at Cambridge

It may be that George's new-found relish for divine verse, indeed, for verse at all, came from his contacts with other students. He would certainly have known Giles Fletcher, especially since Fletcher, like Herbert, was a religious poet, whose poem 'Christs Victorie and Triumph' had established him as the chief religious poet of the college.[28] Another notable entrant to the college that year was Charles Chauncy who would go, like so many Trinity men, to the New World. He was eventually to become the second president of Harvard.[29] Among the friends he made during his Cambridge years, however, two men stand out who would profoundly influence his life: John Williams and Nicholas Ferrar.

'Nick Ferrar' was an undergraduate at Clare College, a man with whom George must have felt an immediate affinity. He, like George, was frail in health. Like George, he was a man of many talents, combined with a real and deep piety. Ferrar had dedicated himself to God's service when he was at school. One night he woke, went downstairs and out into the garden behind the school. There, weeping bitterly, he threw himself down onto the grass and prayed to God for 'guidance and enlightenment'. Suddenly, he knew great peace of mind and, doubts resolved, he knelt and dedicated himself to God's service.[30]

Ferrar was only a year older than George, but he had already been at Cambridge for four years by the time Herbert arrived, having entered university when he was only thirteen.[31] In the end, ill-health forced Ferrar to leave Cambridge in 1613. He was to go on to be involved in the Virginia Company and eventually found the religious community at Little Gidding. It was to Nicholas Ferrar that, from his deathbed, George committed his poetry and Ferrar saw it through publication. Ferrar, too, wrote the first biographical account of Herbert–the preface to *The Temple*, published in 1633.

While their friendship probably blossomed after their years at Cambridge, it was at Trinity that George first made the acquaintance of Ferrar. There are many parallels between their lives–too many to believe that each did not learn from the other's example. Although most of the firm evidence of their relationship has been lost, if there was one man above all others from whom George learnt, it was Nick Ferrar of Clare College.

In his dealings with the church, George was to turn to Ferrar for spiritual help and John Williams for practical help. Williams was in many ways, the complete opposite of Nicholas Ferrar. During Herbert's time at Cambridge, he was Junior Proctor of St John's College from 1611 onwards. He was typical of the statesmen-churchmen of the sixteenth and seventeenth century, and was later to become Lord Keeper of the Privy Seal, Bishop of Lincoln and Archbishop of York.[32]

Williams was a strange mixture, a man who managed to combine the life of a scheming, occasionally unscrupulous, cunning courtier with high clerical rank. He must be one of the few Archbishops ever to be thrown into the Tower for betraying official secrets. During his time in the Tower he never once went to chapel or took communion. When he was Bishop of Lincoln he never once set foot in his own cathedral, instead choosing to entertain with great largesse at his palace in Buckden.[33]

Nevertheless, he was also a great friend and protector of Nicholas Ferrar and his community at Little Gidding–almost as if, by supporting the community, he was doing penance for his own shortcomings. And when Herbert came to take the decision to enter the church, it was Williams who smoothed the path and enabled Herbert to proceed quickly.[34]

In their own way, the two men are symbolic of the two aspects of Cambridge which Herbert experienced. Cambridge not only brought George into contact with the piety of men such as Ferrar, it also brought him into contact with the glittering prize of the Royal Court, peopled by those such as Williams.

'WITHOUT FAVOUR NONE WILL KNOWE YOU, AND WITH IT
YOU WILL NOT KNOWE YOUR SELFE.'
Outlandish Proverbs No.159

Academic Achievements 1615-1618

Herbert took his BA degree in 1613. In the *Order Senioritatis*, which ranked scholars according to merit, Herbert is listed as second in his year with Hacket sixth and Walsingham Shirley eighteenth. On 3 October 1613 he was sworn a minor fellow, proceeding to become a major fellow on 15 March 1615.[35] During this time he would have served, as Hacket did, as a tutor to a number of students.

The following year he became a *sublaector quartae classis* at Trinity. The sublectors were elected for one-year terms to assist the head lecturer (the *Lector Primarius*). There were four sublectors, each lecturing in Greek, Latin, mathematics and Greek grammar.[36]

He was obviously an able lecturer, since the following year, he received the first of his official university posts, one of the four 'Barnaby lecturers' chosen on St Barnabas' day on 11 June. The lectureships had been established by Sir Robert Rede. Herbert was selected to lecture on rhetoric. He was to expound in English on classical authors, such as Cicero and Quintillian, mainly for the benefit of first-year students.[37]

Simonds D'Ewes recalled Herbert as one of the lecturers who had the most impact on him:

Nor was my increase in knowledge small, which I attained

by the ear as well as by the eye, by being present at the public commencements, at Mr. Downes his public Greek lectures, and Mr. Harbert's public rhetoric lectures in the University.[38]

Hacket also comments on Herbert's choice of texts upon which to lecture, for, at least once he used a speech of King James as his text:

> Mr. *George Herbert* being Praelector in the Rhetorique School in *Cambridge* anno 1618 Pass'd by those fluent Orators, that Domineered in the Pulpits of *Athens* and *Rome*, and insisted to Read upon an Oration of King *James*, which he Analysed, shew'd the concinnity of the Parts, the propriety of the Phrase, the height and power of it to move Affections, the Style utterly unknown to the Ancients, who could not conceive what Kingly Eloquence was, in respect of which, those noted Demagogi were but Hirelings, and Triobulary Rhetoricians.[39]

As Amy Charles has pointed out, the context of this shows that Hacket was not necessarily being critical of Herbert, but the fact that Hacket did not criticise Herbert need not blind us to the calculated nature of Herbert's choice. James I had always been interested in the university. Ever since his journey south to accept the crown in that plague-ridden year of 1603, when a deputation of scholars had travelled to meet him at Hinchingbrooke (where he was staying with Sir Oliver Cromwell, uncle of the future Protector) relations between the university and the King had been extremely cordial.[40] James always fancied himself as an academic, and the university made sure that they reinforced this impression. The King often visited Newmarket or Royston, and several times visited the university itself. Each time, significantly, he stayed in Herbert's college, Trinity, establishing the custom that Royal visitors should always be put up by the college.[41]

By now, Herbert had been at the university for nine years. It was time to start thinking of the future. He would have known only too well of James' interest in the universities, and he was playing all the cards he could. Later on in his career he would be in a position to make more of an impact on James, but for now, using the King's work as a model of great rhetoric was the best he could do. All of which shows that if Herbert had dedicated his poetic talents to God, he was a very long way from fully dedicating the rest of his life.

'THE LOVE OF MONEY AND THE LOVE OF LEARNING RARELY MEET.'
Jacula Prudentum No.1168

Financial Problems

First in his mind must have been his financial position. With these appointments his income had risen a little, from the quarterly payments of 3s. 4d. to £2 13s. 4d. yearly. Apart from this, his only source of income was the £30 which his brother Edward had agreed to pay him.[42] For anything else he needed he had to rely on the generosity of his family.

The first letter we have to his step-father Sir John Danvers has been dated by Hutchinson at 1617. However, to judge by the tone, it probably comes from earlier in Herbert's university career. The letter thanks Sir John for the gift of a horse. For a Cambridge undergraduate a horse of his own would have been a boon—horseless undergraduates had to hire horses from Hobson the carrier, where they had no choice of animal but had to take the horse from the stall next the door. Hence the expression, Hobson's choice.[43]

The letter is warm and grateful and promises 'obedience' to his step-father, a promise which hardly reads like the words of a twenty-four-year-old university lecturer. It is also evident from the letter that the horse is the response to one of Herbert's first requests to Sir John—'only hereafter I will take heed how I propose my desires to you, since I find you so willing to yield to my requests'.[44] It can hardly be credited that Herbert would have been eight years at university before he discovered how speedily Sir John responded to his requests. I would tend to put this letter somewhat earlier, therefore, probably in the years between 1609 and 1613 when Herbert was studying for his BA.

The second letter to Sir John, however, is dated 18 March 1617 and here the tone is totally different. There is no talk of obedience; instead Herbert seems almost angry:

Sir,

    I dare no longer be silent, least while I think I am
modest, I wrong both my self, and also the confidence my
Friends have in me; wherefore I will open my case unto
you, which I think deserves the reading at the least; and it
is this, I want Books extremely; You know Sir, how I am
now setting foot into Divinity, to lay the platform of my
future life, and shall I then be fain alwayes to borrow
Books, and build on anothers foundation? What Trades-
man is there who will set up without his Tools? Pardon my
boldness Sir, it is a most serious Case...[45]

He goes on to say that his annuity is barely enough 'to keep me
in health...You know I was sick last Vacation, neither am I yet
recovered, so that I am fain ever and anon, to buy somewhat
tending towards my health.'[46] Herbert's illness was making him
more forward than perhaps he might have been, but there is a
sense of frustration in this letter that he has to make do, he has to
scrimp and save in order to afford the tools of his trade. George
had clearly been ill for some time (the opening to a letter to his
brother Henry written in 1618 jokes, 'The disease which I am
troubled with now is the shortness of time', which only confirms
that his family were not strangers to news of his ailments) and the
letter tells of several trips to Newmarket where Herbert lay 'a day
or two for fresh Air'.[47]
    The other aspect of this letter which has excited biographical
comment is the avowed intention to 'set foot into Divinity', but
this talks of studying divinity, not joining the church. Admittedly, the one often implied the other, especially in the academic
world, but the example of Williams should be enough to show
that not everyone who studied divinity was a stranger to the world
of the Court and the university. And soon, the post of University
Orator was to become vacant.

9

Cambridge

'A FLATTERERS THROAT IS AN OPEN SEPULCHER.'
Outlandish Proverbs No.588

The University Orator

Herbert must have known that the post of University Orator was to become available soon after he assumed the role of Barnaby Lecturer in 1618. He had already acted in the Orator's role in January of that year, when he had written an official letter to Buckingham when he was made a Marquess.

The role of University Orator was really that of a PR man for the university. It was the Orator's duty to write official letters on behalf of the university, make Latin orations on the occasions of official visits to the university and generally to pay compliments to those the university wanted to praise. In many ways he was an academic courtier; he had no choice over who was honoured, he merely had to carry out the task.

To George, writing to Sir John Danvers in September 1619, the Orator's role seemed a highly attractive prize:

> The Orator's place (that you may understand what it is) is the finest place in the University, though not the gainfullest ... but the commodiousness is beyond the Revenue; for the Orator writes all the University Letters, makes all the Orations, be it to King, Prince, or whatever comes to the University; to requite these pains, he takes place next the Doctors, is at all their Assemblies and Meetings, and sits above the Proctors, is Regent or Non-regent at his pleasure, and such like Gaynesses, which will please a young man well.[1]

In the same letter he says that he is presently to make 'an Oration to the whole University of an hour long in *Latin*'. The oration must have gone well, for the month after his letter he was appointed Deputy Orator when the university gave the incumbent Orator, Sir Francis Nethersole, a leave of absence.

Herbert's pursuit of the Orator's post brings into focus one of the central questions about his life, a question which can be paraphrased as: 'Did he jump or was he pushed?' Did he, as Walton claimed, find his court hopes dashed and therefore turn to the church? Or was he, as Amy Charles claimed, always determined to become a priest?

In this letter, Herbert talks solely about the 'glamour' and 'honour' of being Orator. He wants to 'get this place without all your *London* helps...not but that I joy in your favours, but that you may see, that if all fail, yet I am able to stand on mine own legs.'[2] It is not the letter of someone determined on the priestly vocation, but rather the voice of the young man that Walton describes:

> If, during this time he exprest any Error, it was, that he
> kept himself too much retir'd, and at too great a distance
> with all his inferiours: and his cloaths seem'd to prove, that
> he put too great a value on his parts and Parentage.[3]

The letter reflects this pride. It is the letter of one who cares about his own self-esteem, whose concern is with the stature of the job, who looks forward to taking his place among the doctors and to enjoying the 'Gaynesses, which will please a young man well'.

The idea, therefore, that Herbert was from the first set on a religious life simply does not fit with the paths he chose to take along the way. If he had wanted to become a parish priest he could have left university and taken orders at any time after taking his BA. The fact is that throughout his life George Herbert took every opportunity to divert from the priesthood. The Orator's post was well-known to be a stepping-stone to positions of state, as indeed it had proved to be for Nethersole and his predecessor, Sir Robert Naunton. Even when Herbert finally became a deacon it was largely because the statutes of the university required him to take that step, and when other lines of work had been tried and discarded. Even then, he did not proceed to full ordination, and scarcely went near the church into which he was inducted.

Yet the opposite theory–that Herbert only turned to the priesthood after his court hopes were disappointed–is equally flawed. For there is always another side to Herbert. As in his poetry, there was always an inner voice that seemed to be calling him, or nagging at him about the path he was not choosing. Others had recognised this, including Sir Francis Nethersole, the outgoing Orator who expressed some concern about Herbert taking the post:

> I understand by Sir *Francis Nethersols* Letter, that he fears
> I have not fully resolved of the matter, since this place
> being civil may divert me too much from Divinity, at
> which, not without cause, he thinks, I aim; but I have
> wrote him back, that this dignity, hath no such earthiness
> in it, but may very well be joined with Heaven.[4]

The last sentence is significant and perhaps reveals something of the truth behind his actions. One part of George obviously felt that he should be somehow 'joined with Heaven', but the other side, the young man who wanted to be pleased with 'gaynesses', wanted to go the other way. Herbert was prepared to dedicate his poetic gifts to God, but dedicating his career was another matter. He felt he ought to fully commit himself, but the lure of court and society was–at least during his Cambridge days–too much. Perhaps, then, that commitment could be put off until later. In the end, this indecision proved costly. The majority of George's life was spent in a no-man's land of indecision between these two opposing desires. Too much of his short life was spent trying to square the circle, trying to find a way to be joined both with heaven and earth.

Certainly at this stage of his life, the lure of the Orator's post was too strong. His campaign to succeed Sir Francis Nethersole was successful and, on Friday 21 January 1620, at a meeting in the Senate house he was elected to the post, presented with his Orator's habit, book and lamp, and took his place, as he had written, 'next the Doctors'.

'PRAISE NONE TOO MUCH, FOR ALL ARE FICKLE.'
Outlandish Proverbs No.774

Herbert's reputation

In a letter to his successor, Robert Creighton, Herbert gives the best illustration of his approach to the rôle. First and foremost, the Orator has to remember that he is not writing or speaking personally, but on behalf of the university. 'Many things will be fitting for my friend Creighton, which for Alma Mater will be incongruous and out of character.' Creighton is advised to picture the university as a 'matron, holy, reverend, of antique and august countenance'. She is not, therefore, to be decorated with 'stainings of the eyes and painting of the cheeks'. Herbert goes on to recommend that an oration should be 'clear, transparent, lucid...in fine, lest I myself too should transgress, let thy mode of speech be terse and compact'. He warns against too much learning, 'An oration is one thing, a letter is another. Be sparing of learning in letters; in making an oration indulge in it a little— not much even then; for it is not befitting (the character of) our Matron, whom it is thy place to set off to advantage.'[5]

This letter, like all the written or spoken work of the University Orator, was in Latin, English being considered too uncouth a language for fine usage. It was not Herbert's poetic skills, therefore, but his fluency in the classical languages that won him the post. Insofar as he had a poetic reputation at this time at all it was as a writer of Greek and Latin verses, as a witty creator of epigrams, or as a translator. Indeed, it was to Herbert the Latin scholar that Francis Bacon paid the compliment of dedicating his *Translation of Certaine Psalmes into English*, for Herbert had assisted Bacon in translating his *Advancement of Learning* into Latin.[6]

It was in Latin therefore that, shortly after assuming the post, Herbert delivered his first official letter. The letter was to King James, thanking him for the gift of his *Opera Latina*. 'Scotland was too narrow for thee to be able fully to unfold thy wings from the nest,' it gushes. 'What didst thou do thereupon? Thou didst take possession of all the British Isles.'[7] Attached to the letter was a Latin epigram asserting that if a visitor came to Cambridge looking for a library like the Vatican or the Bodleian, then the book would suffice, for the King's book was a library in itself.[8]

The epigram, though over-the-top even by the Court's excessive standards, had the desired effect. James was reported to have expressed an interest in this new orator.

Herbert's work as an Orator and official correspondent may seem to us trivial and sycophantic, but to the university it was vital and extremely practical. His job was to protect the university's interests. Letters were written to major statesmen, especially when they entered into a new office, to tactfully remind them of their links and obligations to Cambridge. His letter to Buckingham for example, written ostensibly to congratulate him on becoming a Marquess, recognises that George Villiers was the voice of King James:

> Through thee, our James shines upon us, thou dost display
> him to the people; and inasmuch as thou thyself art on the
> top of the tree, with one hand thou dost lay upon the King,
> and the other thou dost stretch out to us, clinging to the
> roots.[9]

To Thomas Coventry, on his appointment as Attorney General, Herbert was a little more blatant. 'But if while thou appliest thyself to thy office, any legal matter touching us should occur, do thou set us free, who are occupied with books and with eternity, from such trivial and temporary concerns.'[10] One such major concern was the attempt of the London booksellers to obtain a monopoly on the sale of imported books, something which would have cost the university dear. Herbert wrote to the newly appointed Archbishop of Canterbury on 29 January 1620, 'For they say that the London booksellers, having an eye to their own advantage rather than to that of the public...are longing for certain monopolies, from which circumstance we fear that the prices of the books will be increased, and our privileges diminished.' Bacon, likewise, was entreated to stop this pernicious scheme.[11]

One letter from this time stands out as markedly different in tone from the rest. This was written to Lancelot Andrewes and is a much more personal letter than one written on behalf of the university. Written when he was just taking up the Orator's post, the letter uses 'I' throughout. Herbert has obviously just returned from seeing the new Bishop of Winchester, 'At once from the comfort of thy countenance, I grown greater and fuller for joy, returned to Cambridge...Now buried in academic affairs, unwillingly I cut down my time to these things.' Herbert talks of being like Andrewes, but in terms of his learning rather than his piety. He also talks of the business of his life, as at this time he was filling both the Orator's post and lecturing in rhetoric: 'I am discharging two important functions among my fellow collegians–that of Professor of Rhetoric for this year, and of Orator for more years than one...'[12]

It was Herbert's Latin skill, therefore, that was valuable to the university. Latin was the 'official' language, the language of encomium and diplomacy. Herbert's fluency in this language, and his rhetorical and persuasive skills, were what really established his reputation at the university. Indeed, his first published poetry was not the English verses aimed at heaven, but two Latin poems aimed squarely at earth. Throughout his time at Cambridge, Herbert had written occasional verse in Latin. On 6 November 1612, Prince Henry, eldest son of James I, died of typhoid fever. Herbert wrote two memorial poems in Latin, 'In Obitum Henrici Principis Walliae', which were included in the memorial volume *Epicedium Cantabrigiense*. Another of his Latin poems was included in a memorial volume to James' wife, Queen Anne, on her death in 1619.[13]

Before that, however, Herbert had contributed two poems to an anthology presented to Frederick, Elector Palatine, when he visited the university in 1613. Frederick had just married Elizabeth, daughter of James I. He visited Cambridge with his brother-in-law Prince Charles. Herbert's predecessor as Orator, Sir Francis Nethersole, welcomed them and presented them with 'a written book of verses, fairly bound in vellum filleted and guilded, with crimson strings...'[14] Frederick's volume was lost until it was rediscovered in the Vatican Library in 1962. It contained two Latin poems by Herbert, one commemorating the visit of Elector Frederick and the other celebrating his marriage to Queen Elizabeth.[15]

At the time, the marriage seemed full of glittering and glorious promise. Frederick was one of the principal Protestant princes in Europe, and it seemed that the two of them would form a splendid court. A few years later, however, the Bohemian Estates deposed their king and asked Frederick to take his place.

Unwisely, Frederick agreed and journeyed to Prague to become the King of Bohemia. He was to enjoy his throne for little more than a year. A Protestant king in the heart of Europe was more than the Catholics could stand. They dispatched a united force under Tilly to drive the King out. Frederick's reign as King of Bohemia lasted just over a year, before defeat at the battle of the White Hill forced him to flee Prague for exile in Holland.

When the adventure was over, and Elizabeth was living in exile, Herbert wrote another poem to the Queen. The poem – a paean of praise to Queen Elizabeth – is unusual in that Herbert did not write it in Latin, the language of flattery, but in English. Fluent in six languages, with a keen wit, Elizabeth had the grace that only comes from having endured and conquered hardship. She was widowed at an early age, and lost her eldest son in a swimming accident in the Zuyder Zee. It would be hard to overpraise such a woman, but in this poem Herbert manages it, with magnificent unctuousness. The poem is self-consciously clever, full of outlandish compliments and classical allusions. It can be dated with accuracy to 1621-1622, when Elizabeth was living in Holland in exile.

We cannot know for sure why Herbert wrote the poem – it may have been part of his official duties as Orator. More likely, it was a personal attempt to gain preferment. Others of his friends and acquaintances, after all, had gained through association with the 'Queen of Hearts' as Elizabeth was known. Nicholas Ferrar had accompanied the Court as a gentleman-in-waiting soon after the marriage in 1613 (although he did not travel to Prague on their ill-fated venture).[16]

Similarly, George's predecessor as Orator, Sir Francis Nether-sole, was appointed English Secretary to the Electress, a post he filled for almost fifteen years.[17] There can be no other explanation for this poem than that Herbert was complimenting the Queen with a view to possible employment.

'PARDONS AND PLEASANTNESSE ARE GREAT REVENGES OF
SLANDERS.'
Outlandish Proverbs No.365

Musae Responsoriae

Far from reserving his poetic gifts for the use of God, therefore,
Herbert used them throughout his Cambridge years to praise and
flatter Kings, Queens and other nobility. There are, of course,
certain exceptions. *Passio Discerpta* is a long poem concentrating
on the passion of Christ which may well (as Amy Charles suggests) have been composed as a Lenten meditation. *Lucus* is an
anthology of Latin epigrams and verses on a variety of topics.[18]
However, both these poems are more akin to Latin exercises than
the heartfelt expressions of Herbert's English verse. Even the
long set of Latin verses, the *Musae Responsoriae*, although written
about a religious subject are really an attempt to make an impression on the powers-that-be.

The *Musae Responsoriae* are a poetic reply to an earlier set of
Latin verses, Andrew Melville's *Anti-Tami-Cami-Categoria*.
Melville was a Puritan critic: 'a Minister of the Scotch Church,
and Rector of St. *Andrews*; who, by a long and constant Converse,
with a discontented part of that Clergy which oppos'd Episco-
pacy, became at last to be a chief leader of that faction'.[19] He was
'a man of an unruly wit, of a "strange confidence", of so furious a
Zeal, and of so ungovern'd passions, that his insolence to the
King...caus'd him to be committed prisoner to the Tower of
London: Where he remained very angry for three years.' *Anti-
Tami-Cami-Categoria* was an attack on the rites of the Church of
England, which, among other things, compared a set liturgy to
magic incantations, and the words of a priest at baptism to the
sound of a screech owl.[20]

Anti-Tami-Cami-Categoria was not published until 1620,
although it was composed many years earlier. Walton's assertion
that Herbert composed these verses while at Westminster School
is unlikely, even if Melville's poems had been circulated in manuscript form. It is far more probable that it was the first printing
of Melville's 'malicious bitter Verses against our *Liturgy*, our
Ceremonies, and our *Church-governments*' which occasioned Herbert's response. A date of 1620 also fits better with the tone of the
poem and the fact that it is dedicated to King James, Prince

Charles and Lancelot Andrewes, then Bishop of Winchester. Amy Charles suggests that the poem was not an attempt to gain royal or ecclesiastical favour, and that it was not intended 'for the public eye'. To which one might reasonably enquire: Why was it written at all? The fact is that everything about the poem is an attempt to impress. Herbert may very well have been motivated by a concern to defend the church in which he had been brought up, but the tenor of the poem is not one of a disciple defending his doctrine but of a schoolboy showing off. His dedication to James sets the tone:

> Caesar, before the light
> Of your grace and attention was opened to me,
> My muse too was vile mud:
> But now, because of you, she is alive,
> She can creep along, and has the nerve
> To step up where you are the sun.[21]

It is difficult to agree with the esteem in which the *Musae Responsoriae* were held in the seventeenth century. Herbert's verses are an exhibitionist display of schoolboy smugness. Although dealing with a religious subject, the *Musae Responsoriae* are not religious verses but a collection of verbal pyrotechnics designed to gain the approval of those to whom they were dedicated.

'KNOWLEDGE IS FOLLY, EXCEPT GRACE GUIDE IT.'
Outlandish Proverbs No.248

English Poetry

The fact that Herbert was writing such verses in Latin does not mean that he was entirely neglecting his English verse. The problem is that dating Herbert's English poetry is a hazardous and largely conjectural task. There have been many attempts to fix a chronology of his religious poems, but the only ones which we can date with any certainty are the sonnets sent to his mother in the New Year of 1610.

We can, however, assign some poems to two different periods of Herbert's life, from the fact that he made two collections at different times. The earliest collection is generally known as W (from the fact that it was deposited in Dr Williams' Library in London) and contains seventy-seven poems as well as 'L'Envoy' and 'The Dedication'. In all probability W is partially written in Herbert's own hand and is probably his own first attempt at sorting and editing his poems, selecting from the entire body of his work.

The second collection, known as B, is in the Bodleian Library at Oxford and contains 163 poems.[22] B was written by scribes at Little Gidding, copied from the manuscript sent to Nicholas Ferrar by Herbert on his death-bed. B is a later expansion and amendment of W, so we can be reasonably certain that poems found in B and not in W come from a later period.[23] Deciding precisely when these collections were made is a matter of guess-work. B was probably made at Bemerton, towards the end of his life, so it is likely that all the additions in the collection come from those years. W was probably compiled after Herbert had left Cambridge, but could very well have been chosen from material written throughout the seventeen years he spent at university. It is likely that, throughout his time as Orator, Herbert was writing not only fulsome Latin verses but also many of the English poems for which he was to become famous.

Two poems, especially, suggest themselves as earlier works. 'The Church Porch' and 'The Church Militant', are long poems of a type that Herbert rarely attempted. Of 'The Church Porch', Hutchinson suggests that, 'Herbert began this poem early and often revised it.'[24] The tone is clearly that of an elder brother writing to a younger. It is addressed to a young man, like Herbert, a man whose 'sweet youth and early hopes inhance/Thy rate and price, and mark thee for a treasure.'[25] It has a notably didactic tone, and indeed is intended as a kind of primer for life, a series of moralities and precepts for one who would not listen to sermons. The poem preaches against lust (stanzas 2-4), drunkenness (5-9), swearing (10-12), lying (13), idleness (14-15), debt and expense (26-31), gambling (33-34), and so on—all sins to which young men are particularly prone.

The poem speaks disparagingly of 'forrain' wisdom. In W, stanza 62 begins 'leave not thine owne deere-cuntry-cleanlines ffor this ffrench sluttery.'[26] Although omitted from the later version, this would seem to hint that the poem was written for

George's younger brother Henry, who spent much time in France from 1615 onwards.

There exists a letter from George to Henry, which Hutchinson assigns to the year 1618 but which could just as easily have been written for Henry's earlier visit. In the letter Herbert claims he is too busy 'to impart unto you some of those observations which I have framed to myself in conversation; and where of I would not have you ignorant. As I shal find occasion, you shal receive them by peeces.' 'The Church Porch' may well be the 'peeces' in which this advice was imparted.

The letter advises Henry to take to heart all that is best in France, to transport 'French commodities to your own country'. It advises Henry to be proud, 'not with a foolish vanting of yourself when there is no caus, but by setting a just price of your qualities'.[27] Such advice accords well with Walton's depiction of Herbert as a proud young man, 'at too great a distance with all his inferiours'. The letter ends with a PS: 'My brother is somewhat of the same temper and is perhaps a little more mild, but you will hardly perceive it.' Edward was being difficult.

'The Church Militant' is similar to 'The Church Porch', but instead of moralities and mottos, it aims at a lengthy and somewhat cumbersome history of the spread of the Christian religion and the way it has been dogged by sin. It is most notable for its emphasis on the potential of America:

> Religion stands on tip-toe in our land,
> Readie to passe to the *American* strand.[28]

This reflected the optimistic view at the time that America, and particularly the British colony of Virginia, was to be the new Jerusalem. It was a hope that was to be cruelly dashed in later years. Herbert could not have written with such optimism after the collapse of the Virginia Company in 1624, so it is safe to assume that this long poem is an early work. Either way, Herbert did not pursue the format. Perhaps he recognised that, despite his fondness for proverbs, he was never at his best as a moralist.

10

1619-1624

Cambridge, Paris, Holland, Spain

'THERE ARE THREE WAIES, THE UNIVERSITIES, THE SEA,
THE COURT.'
Outlandish Proverbs No.383

Herbert's Family

Herbert had only held his MA for five years when in 1620 he
became Orator. The University Statutes stated that a Master of
Arts who was the Public Orator had precedence over all others of
that rank.[1] Herbert had therefore achieved status and honour and
a post from which he could reasonably expect preferment. It is
clear, however, that the post soon began to pall on him. As Amy
Charles states, 'In all the Epistolae [the official letters written by
Herbert as University Orator] Herbert strikes few notes that are
anything but conventional courtesy.'[2]

In his first eighteen months as Orator he wrote thirteen official
letters, but after a letter to the Lord Treasurer in October 1621 the
supply dries up. Herbert by that time had tired of the Orator's
post and the flattery it entailed; the novelty had worn off, and
there was scant sign of court preferment. We know little of his
activities between 1622 and 1624. He was still at Cambridge, he
still delivered some orations, but he had stopped writing official
letters. His attitudes were changing as well. Other factors, most
notably the experiences of his family, had begun to sour his view
of court life.

'HONOUR AND PROFIT LIE NOT IN ONE SACKE.'
Outlandish Proverbs No.232

Edward Herbert

Firstly there was the experience of his eldest brother, Sir Edward.
Throughout the decade 1609-1619, Edward had lived the life of a
professional soldier. He had fought at the Battle of Juliers and in
the Low Countries during the long, wearisome tangle of conflicts
that became known as the Thirty Years War. So protracted were
these wars that they became a regular fixture in the lives of young
British noblemen. Wrote Basil Willey:

> A nobleman's son could accompany one of the great Sea
> Captains to the Spanish Main, or he could fight in the Low
> Countries. Indeed, the wars in the Low Countries in the
> first half of the seventeenth century, amounted to a
> standing social resource for the English aristocracy; they
> were a normally recurring fixture in the seventeenth
> century season, analogous to Ascot, Cowes or the 12th
> August in modern high life.[3]

Showing the talent for languages that all Herberts seemed to
possess, Edward taught himself French, Italian and Spanish with
the aim of '[making] myself a citizen of the world as far as it were
possible'.[4] He travelled throughout Europe, first with his friend
Aurelian Townsend and then on his own.

While he was abroad, he also discovered the delights of the
duel. Duelling was so fashionable as to be almost a craze in
France at that time. One contemporary account records that
between 1606-1609 nearly 2,500 French noblemen lost their lives
in duels.[5] For Edward, already hot-headed and quick to take
offence, the duel was an irresistible temptation. His *Autobiography*
is full of real and imagined slights, challenges issued and
duels fought, both at home and abroad. That he was handsome
did not help, for ladies were always falling in love with him and
one jealous husband at least even went to the extent of ambushing
him with four men. Edward won the fight against the odds and
immediately sent a further challenge to the enraged husband.[6]
Needless to say, he always denied the charge.

'Noe man vnderstood the vse of his weapon better than I did or hath more dextrously prevailed himselfe thereof on all occasions,' he wrote in his *Autobiography*.[7] However, despite this willingness to fight, fate nearly always cheated Edward of the chance of showing his bravery. As Willey says, 'It happened repeatedly, either that his adversary failed to turn up, or that authority interposed to prevent the fight.'[8]

He had returned home to England seriously ill with the fever in 1617, 'so lean and yellow, that scarce any man did know me'.[9] Then in 1619 high honour came to Edward. James appointed him ambassador to France.

It was probably the most important ambassadorial post available. At first glance it seems a strange appointment, for on the surface at least Edward does not seem the most diplomatic of people. (The appointment certainly came as a surprise to Edward, who thought that the Privy Council had sent for him to answer yet another false allegation made against him.)

Nevertheless, he proved an intelligent and able diplomat, in between bouts of taunting the Spanish ambassador and 'some follies, which I afterwards repented and do still repent of'.[10] He took up residence in Paris, where he was known as a fanatical Protestant. For a little time, his younger brother Henry joined him as a secretary.

'FOR THE SAME MAN TO BE AN HERETICK AND A GOOD
SUBJECT IS, INCOMPOSSIBLE.'
Jacula Prudentum No.1058

De Veritate

If his travels introduced him to the duel, they also introduced him to something equally dangerous, albeit spiritually; the fashion of irreligion. On his first visit to France he had lodged for a while with 'that incomparable scholar Isaac Casaubon'. Casaubon was a humanist scholar in a country riven by religious dissension, and Edward's exposure to the thought of this man was to have a lasting effect on his life. He had also stayed with the Montmorency family who were members of the 'Politiques'–a political group which supported toleration for Protestants and which attracted many liberal thinkers.[11]

It was during his time at Paris that Edward wrote *De Veritate*, the book on which his reputation as a philosopher rests and the achievement of which he was most proud. It is, as the name implies, a search for truth. Edward had begun the book while ill in London in 1617, the same year that Herbert began his serious studies in theology; but the two lines of enquiry could hardly have been further apart. While George was defending the Church against Andrew Melville's attacks, Edward was writing one of the earliest works of rationalism, applying independent examination of the facts. He rejects appeals to tradition or authority, 'defends the freedom of the individual, and limits the value of revelation to its first-hand witness'.[12]

De Veritate was written against a background of religious conflict. The wars between Catholics and Protestants had moved from Prague and Bohemia to the Low Countries and showed little signs of abating. It was hardly surprising, therefore, that some sceptics began to wish a plague on both their houses. Among those who attempted to formulate a generalised theory of Christianity was Hugo Grotius, whose book *De Veritate Religionis Christianae* was published in 1622. Grotius wanted to ground Christianity in tolerance and to establish principles to which all Christians could adhere. Herbert was not writing the same thing at all. Herbert's aim was to find a common ground, not between denominations, but between all religions. Grotius was an ecumenical Christian. Herbert was a deist.

In the final forty pages of the book, Herbert formulates his five 'Common Notions' of religion, the real basis of religion which can be found in 'every instance of ritual, folly, error and fiction'.[13] The elements are that there is a supreme God; that he ought to be worshipped; that the best way of worshipping is 'the practice of vertue'; that man should repent of vices and sins; and that there is punishment or reward after death.[14]

In this day and age, such beliefs sound little different to that of most bishops, but in Herbert's time such thought was more revolutionary. The book is, throughout, a carefully worded attack on organised religion and on Christianity in particular. Of course, he never mentions this specifically–in Jacobean times to do so could bring heavy penalties–but it is implicit throughout his work. From the moment of its publication, Herbert's work was attacked. 'Not acclaim as a forerunner, but scorn as a perverter of religion was Herbert's usual lot.' *De Veritate* was banned by the Catholics and attacked by the Protestants.

The book was finished in 1622. Having finished the manuscript, Edward with typical inconsistency fell to his knees and asked God for a sign as to whether he should publish it. He was answered by a peal of thunder, which he took as a sign that he should go ahead. He dedicated the work to his secretary William Boswell and, most surprisingly, to his brother George.

It is hard to imagine a book more guaranteed to anger and upset George than *De Veritate*. Its entire approach was alien to George's way of thinking. To Edward, man's role was a quest for individual truth:

> The conclusions arrived at in former ages have now come to weigh so heavily upon our own reflections, that there is scarcely anyone in the world who is content to pursue an independent path in the search for truth; every one submits himself to some alien Church or School; thereby wholly renouncing his own powers.[15]

To George, catechising—teaching the received doctrine of the church—was a vital part of his ministry and something he advocated in *The Country Parson*:

> How came this world to be as it is? Was it made, or came it by chance? Who made it? Did you see God make it? Then are there some things to be beleeved that are not seen? Is this the nature of beliefe? Is not Christianity full of such things as are not to be seen, but beleeved?[16]

Faith, the very faith which *De Veritate* spent its pages attacking, was a vital part of George's life. Perhaps in dedicating the book to George, Edward was appealing to his brother as one scholar to another, dedicating to him a work of philosophy which he thought George would appreciate. If so, it appears to be a hamfisted compliment, for few books could be less to George's liking. If it was not a mistake, then the dedication appears in a darker light, as some kind of ironic taunt, or a philosophical practical joke. There is certainly an ironic tone to the wording of the dedication which instructs George to 'expunge anything that [he] might find that is contrary to good morals or the true Catholic faith'.[17]

At least George did not live to read Edward's later work *De Religione Laici* with its *Appendix ad Sacerdotes* (1645) in which Edward attacked priests whom he accused of 'conspiring that neither entering nor leaving this world should be quite lawful without their aid'.[18]

If George disapproved of Edward's religious views, he may well have looked on his earthly career with envy, at least at first. However, Edward's success was not to last. He remained ambassador to France for two years and then, in 1624, suddenly lost favour. The unwillingness of James to support his Protestant son-in-law in the battle for Bohemia bewildered and angered Edward, as did the machinations over the proposed marriage of Prince Charles to the Spanish Infanta. When the match fell through and James turned to France for a suitable bride, Edward was removed from office. He was not to blame. He was merely a victim of James' penchant for keeping his servants in the dark and then sacking them when they bumped into things.

The letter recalling Edward to London was curt and abrupt and signalled the end of Edward's good standing with the Court. What is more, the arrears of his salary were never paid, neither were the expenses he had laid out. For the rest of his long life, he was systematically passed over for public service and honour. James made him Baron of Castle Island, a trivial title, and Charles I made him Lord Herbert of Cherbury, but these ennoblements failed to make up for the many disappointments.

Edward's treatment must have been a salutory lesson for George, for an ambassador was above all else an orator. If pursuing the path of professional oratory meant being discarded by the King and losing your faith to boot, then we can easily imagine why George chose not to pursue that path.

'OLD MEN GO TO DEATH, DEATH COMES TO YOUNG MEN.'
Jacula Prudentum No.1

Other Brothers

The careers of his other brothers must also have had a profound effect on George. Edward, though he tends to concentrate on their military aspects, gives admirable precis of their lives.

Richard had followed Edward to the Low Countries, where:

> He continued many years with much Reputation both in
> the wars and for fighting single Duels, which were many;
> in so much that between both, he carried, as I have been
> told, the scars of four and twenty wounds upon him to his
> grave and lieth buried in Berghenapsoom.[19]

Richard was only 32 when he died in 1622. The next brother, William, was even younger. He went first to Denmark where, 'Fighting a single combat, and having his sword broken, he not only defended himself with that piece which remained, but closing with his adversary threw him down, and so held him untill company came in.'[20] William then followed Richard to the Low Countries, where, presaging the fate of his brother, he was killed in 1617.

In the same year Charles Herbert, fellow of New College Oxford, died. Like his younger brother George, he was a poet and academic, and had 'given great hopes of himself in every way'.[21] Charles rates only one sentence in Edward's *Autobiography*. He never went abroad, he never fought any duels, he died young. No wonder Edward was at a loss what to say about him.

There can be no doubt that the deaths of these young men had a profound effect on George. Charles' death in the cloistered calm of his Oxford college must have reminded him only too well of his own physical frailty. The fate of his bookish brother must have been in his mind especially during 1622, for Herbert was gravely ill in February of that year—far worse than he had ever been before. An undergraduate named Joseph Mede wrote to Sir Martin Stuteville to tell him of the death of the Junior Proctor and that 'Our Orator also they say will not escape being at deaths dore.'[22]

He was absent from meals in Trinity for twelve weeks.[23] He had recovered by May, for he wrote to his mother, who had also been ill. The letter is worth looking at in some detail, for it is a markedly different Herbert who is writing now. Gone are the proud comments about the 'glorie' of his station, now it is all business:

> I wish earnestly that I were again with you: and, would
> quickly make good my wish but that my employment does
> fix me here, it being now but a month to our
> *Commencement*...For my self, *dear Mother*, I alwaies fear'd
> sickness more then death, because sickness hath made me
> unable to perform those Offices for which I came into the
> world, and must yet be kept in it.[24]

He does not say what these offices are, but goes on to tell his
mother not to worry about her children. In essence, he says, they
are old enough to look after themselves. And as for her fears of
the future:

> I beseech you consider all that can happen to you are either
> afflictions of Estate, or Body, or Mind. – For those of
> Estate? of what poor regard ought they to be, since if we
> had Riches we are commanded to give them away: so that
> the best use of them is, having, not to have them. – But
> perhaps being above the Common people, our Credit and
> estimation calls on us to live in a more splendid fashion? –
> but, Oh God! how easily is that answered, when we
> consider that the Blessings in the holy Scripture, are never
> given to the rich, but to the poor. I never find Blessed be
> the Rich; or, Blessed be the Noble; but, *Blessed be the*
> *Meek*, and *Blessed be the Poor*, and, *Blessed be the Mourners*
> *for they shall be comforted*. – And yet, Oh God! most carry
> themselves so, as if they had not only not desir'd, but, even
> fear'd to be blessed.[25]

It was not so long ago that he was complaining of not having
enough money to buy books. The rest of the letter is not unlike
reading a religious tract. It is strewn with Bible references, as
George tells his mother to rejoice in her afflictions, to remember
the sufferings of the martyrs and other such comforting messages.
Clearly Herbert had changed from the proud Orator of 1620.
His illness in 1622, which had so nearly killed him, seems to have
permanently altered his life. His poems, many of which could
easily have been written during this time, talk of illness in terms
of correction and rebuking from God. Throughout his life he was
plagued by illness, and throughout his life he sought to find some
meaning in it. He was not always as successful as he would have

his mother believe in this letter. His poems record his different moods, from the depths of pain and despair, to the heights of religious faith. The Herbert who put the collection of his poems together was a more mature Herbert than our letter-writer, a man who was not afraid to be seen in moments of weakness.

The letter certainly gives the impression of one writing at the height of religious enthusiasm. Herbert was not always to live in those heady regions. His old indecision and quest for power would reassert itself, but it is clear that during this time, his illness had a significant effect on him. Charles even suggests that he wrote the Latin poems *Passio Discerpta* during this time.[26] They would certainly fit with this mood, being almost Ignatian exercises in exploring Christ's suffering.

'HE THAT WILL LEARNE TO PRAY, LET HIM GOE TO SEA.'
Outlandish Proverbs No.84

Thomas Herbert

The disappointments of court life that were so evident in the life of Edward were echoed in the life of the youngest brother. Thomas led perhaps the most adventurous life of all the brothers and was Edward's favourite, if space allocated in the *Autobiography* is anything to go by.

When he was young he was 'sent as a Page to Sir Edward Cecil Lord Generall of his Majesties auxiliary forces to the Princes in Germany'.[27] Thomas then fought alongside his brother Edward at the siege of Juliers in 1610. He then went to sea as an officer, eventually arriving at 'Suratte And from thence went with the Marchants to the greate Mogull where he had stayd aboue a Tweluemoneth he returned with the same Fleete back againe to England'.[28] King James then sent this able young mariner to Algiers to fight pirates, but the expedition was to prove Thomas's first experience of the treachery of state promises; for it was grievously underfunded and the men were 'in greate want of Money and Uictualls'. Thomas fortunately managed to take a ship to the value of '1800 pounds, which it was thought saued the whole Fleete from perishing...' Fresh from this dispiriting and dangerous experience, Thomas's next trip was to command one of the ships which brought the Prince back from Spain.

Like his oldest brother, Thomas's career was full of more promise than results. Although he was to be appointed Captain of the Dreadnought in 1625, he failed to win any high honour and eventually 'retyred to a private and melancholy life, being much discontented to finde others preferred before him'.[29]

'AT COURT, EVERY ONE FOR HIMSELFE.'
Outlandish Proverbs No.795

The Court in the 1620s

The man who appointed Thomas to his only captaincy was George Villiers, first the Earl, then Marquess, then Duke of Buckingham. Buckingham was James' favourite; the ageing monarch was besotted with the man he called his 'Steenie' from his supposed resemblance to St Stephen. Villiers was not only good-looking, but cunning and calculating. He could wind this ageing and increasingly senile king round his little finger. He played along with the King's pathetic simpering, by signing his letters, 'Your Majesty's most humble Slave and Dogge, Steenie'.[30]

Foreign diplomats gossiped of the King's behaviour. The French ambassador wrote:

> The King alone seems free and has made a journey to
> Newmarket, as a certain other sovereign once did to Capri.
> He takes his beloved Buckingham with him, wishes rather
> to be his friend than king, and to associate his name to the
> heroes of friendship in antiquity. Under such specious
> titles he endeavours to conceal scandalous doings, and
> because his strength deserts him for these, he feeds his eyes
> where he can no longer content his other senses. The end
> of all is ever the bottle.[31]

It was not only Stephen to whom Buckingham was compared. 'Christ had his John and I have My George' said James, a phrase which must have shocked his courtiers, used though they were to his obscenities. A man with such habits was not a monarch to whom the deeply religious George Herbert could happily pledge his allegiance.

Herbert would have had opportunity to see first hand what the

King was like, for he visited the university early in 1623 on what was his third visit to Cambridge. He attended a performance of *Loiola*, a Latin play written by Herbert's friend John Hacket. The play was hardly a wild success, but the King did at least laugh 'once or twice toward the end'. Before the King boarded his coach to leave, 'the Orator Mr. Herbert did make a short Farewell Speech unto him'.[32] Once again, Herbert was a success and the King requested a copy of an epigram which he had made.

The old King was fading, however, and Buckingham paid studious attention to the Prince of Wales, Charles. Together they concocted the insane plan to wed Charles to the daughter of the Spanish King, Philip IV. Failing to get an answer from Philip, Buckingham decided that he and the Prince should travel to Spain incognito to press their case. They travelled via Paris where they stayed briefly with Edward. Naturally, the prospect of a marriage between their future king and their ancient Catholic foes enraged and upset the English populace. Perhaps Herbert's opinions were influenced by his visits home, where the vicar of St Martin's-in-the-Fields, John Everard, was so opposed to the match that he preached regularly against it; an action which landed him in jail 'six or seven times'.[33] In the end the expedition ended in failure and disgrace. Buckingham and Charles returned in ignominy, in a fleet of ships, one of which was commanded by Thomas Herbert.[34]

Through his brother Thomas, and from Edward who was still ambassador at the time, George would have discovered first-hand the news of this disgraceful expedition. He would also have known that Charles and Buckingham came back determined on war with Spain, fuelled by their humiliation.

In October 1623 they visited Cambridge together. Herbert, as was customary, delivered the oration; but this time he juxtaposed the normal vacuous compliments with a passionate plea for peace. Reading the speech, one can clearly scent the smoke from burning bridges. Herbert praised Charles for having travelled to Spain, risking his own life, and all for the cause of peace.[35] The Prince is likened to a balm or medicine, to cure the ills of the world, chief among which is war, 'And in this marriage, our most sweet Prince, not only had a view to posterity, but also to the present age, while he desires the peace which we freely enjoy now for so many years in this way to be secured and everlasting.'

Charles, of course, had not gone seeking peace and did not want peace now. He had gone seeking a bride, and when he was rebuffed he and Buckingham returned determined to punish the Spanish.

Herbert had, however, lost two brothers in wars and nearly lost another to starvation in the course of a misguided expedition against pirates. He had already begun to criticise war. In the section of *Lucus* called 'Triumphis Mortis' he asked the question, 'Do we have one life only to kill six hundred?'[36] To enter a war over the failure of an unpopular match must have seemed like lunacy. 'Without peace, all life is storm and the world a desert,' he announced to the Prince. 'In peace, sons bury their fathers–in war, fathers their sons.'[37] His oration even included a criticism of those who benefited from war, 'How cruel is glory which is reared upon the necks of men; where it is doubtful whether he who achieves it, or he who suffers is the more miserable!'[38]

Herbert was not a naïve, ivy-tower academic. He must have known that to praise peace would only anger his audience, but he was not prepared to stay silent this time, even if it meant the loss of his court hopes. As S.R.Gardiner wrote, 'From Charles, rushing headlong into war, the lover of peace had no favour to expect.'[39] Interestingly enough, at the same time that George was offending Charles, Henry was offending James. The King was as firmly opposed to a war with Spain as his son was for it, so to refer to Spain in any context was to play with fire. In 1624, Henry in his role as Master of Revels licensed Middleton's play *A Game at Chess* which satirised the Spanish match and lampooned various public figures. James was extremely annoyed–more so since the play was a huge success–and Henry was hauled before the Star Chamber to explain why he had licensed such a seditious work.[40]

Thus, the years following his appointment as Orator saw a marked change in Herbert's outlook. His illness; the violent deaths of his brothers, William and Richard; the experiences of Thomas; the sad demise of Charles; the ungrateful treatment of Edward and the degeneration of court life under the increasingly senile James; all combined to alter George's outlook.

By 1624, when Edward was recalled in disgrace, George had apparently given up his hopes of court preferment. Which is not to say that he had given up dreams of power and influence, for, if the court was closed to him, there was always Parliament.

Westminster, Chelsea

'ALL COMPLAINE.'
Outlandish Proverbs No.750

Parliament

In the Parliament of 1623-1624, Sir William Herbert, knight, represented the county of Montgomery and George Herbert, gentleman, the borough.[1]

It is not known why George decided to enter Parliament – some have suggested that it was mere necessity, for Edward and Henry were in France, and someone had to take up the family place. But if the Montgomery seat was anyone's 'family' seat, it was that of Herbert's kinsman, William, fourth Earl of Pembroke, who had at least four 'family' seats in his gift, including both of the Montgomery seats, and several in Wiltshire.[2]

Herbert, then, attended Parliament as part of the political bloc organised by the powerful Earl of Pembroke. Even if Herbert was only responding to family duty, he was also making contacts and seeking preferment, albeit through a totally different route. He was not an independent member in Parliament; he was serving his powerful kinsman.

Amy Charles argues that 'delusions about the glories of public office' were not the motivation for Herbert taking his seat in the Commons. 'The fall of his friend Bacon that began with a parliamentary enquiry in 1621 was too recent a reminder,' she writes.[3] But Herbert's allegiance to Pembroke would seem to indicate that he was still interested in power, and in any case Bacon's fall was directly attributable to the increasing influence and power of Parliament itself. Herbert may have given up on the Court, but he was perhaps scenting the faint breath of a new kind of power – the power of a Parliament which was to find its full expression some twenty years later.

Parliament at this time was just setting foot into this turbulent period. It had already provoked James by attacking the increasingly extortionate monopolies system and refusing to subsidise a war. What is more, the revival of the process of impeachment showed that the two Houses—Lords and Commons—were working in deadly harmony. The Commons could indict a member of James' government who would then have to stand trial before the Lords. Such an action destroyed the monopolist Sir Giles Mompesson, and then Bacon.[4]

What took up Herbert's time during the Parliament of 1624, however, was the crisis in the affairs of the Virginia Company, a crisis which demonstrated how far short of full power Parliament was.

'A GARDEN MUST BE LOOKT UNTO AND DREST AS THE BODY.'
Outlandish Proverbs No.129

The House at Chelsea

During his spell in Parliament, George probably lived at the family house in Charing Cross. This house passed to the ownership of Edward in 1617, when his mother and step-father had moved to a new house in Chelsea. Magdalene Herbert had now been married for fifteen years. There is every indication that it was a successful and happy relationship. However, by 1624, she was ill, in the illness that Donne was to refer to in his memorial sermon:

> And for her, some sicknesses, in the declination of her
> yeeres, had opened her to an overflowing of *Melancholie*;
> Not that she ever lay under that *water*, but yet, had
> sometimes, some high Tides of it.[5]

From 1617 she would have been able to escape these moods of melancholy by retreating to their house in the village of Chelsea which was eventually to become their main residence, with the Charing Cross house as their town house. Amy Charles is wrong to suggest they moved there in 1609, for the earliest evidence of Sir John having property at Chelsea is in an enquiry from the third Earl of Lincoln about 'a certain Portion of Land in Chelsey Called the Moorehouse Purchased by my Lord my father for one Mr Roper wth I haue sold to Sr John Da[n]vers...'^6

The Moorehouse was not, despite a story recorded by Aubrey, the house where Sir Thomas More had lived, but it may have been built by him. Sir John spent much time and energy in making the house habitable, which may account for the fact that the actual deed of conveyance was not agreed until 1622/23, in accordance with 'covenants and agreements' made some five years earlier.^7

The house faced south, towards the river. Entrance to the house was gained through a gateway flanked by two brick 'Pyramides'. 'As you sitt at dinner in the Hall,' wrote Aubrey, who has left us a detailed description of the house and garden, 'you are entertaind with two delightfull Vista's: one southward over the Thames & to Surrey: the other northward into that curious Garden...' On the east side of the hall there was a little 'Chappell or Oratorie, finely painted: next by it a Drawing-roome, whose Floor is checquered, like a Chess-board, wth Box and Eugh [Yew] pannels of about six inches square.'^8

It was the garden, however, which was famous and which was laid out in a style introduced to England by Sir John. Aubrey wrote that 'the Pleasure and Use of Gardens were unknown to our great Grandfathers: They were contented with Pot-herbs: and did mind chiefly their Stables... 'Twas Sir John Danvers of Chelsey (Brother and Heir to Henry Danvers Earle of Danby) who first taught us the way of Italian gardens.'^9

The garden was full of statues and figures, mainly of shepherds and shepherdesses. There was a 'Boscage' or wilderness of 'Lilac's, Syringa's &c.(Sweet Briar &c. Holly-Juniper): and about 4 or 5 Apple trees and peare trees... The east and west ends of this little darke, shadie Boscage delivered you into the stately great gravelled Walkes of the garden, East & West.'^10

Between the two walks there was an 'Ovall Bowling-green' and in the north of the garden was a curious building:

> So at the north part of the garden here the earth is
> excavated in the shape of a Wedge...where at the bottom

(which is as deep as ye Thames) is a round Well or
Basin... over this flatt-square (where the Well is) is a high
arch of 25-30 foot up over (above) which is a fine
Banquetting roome: the windowes whereof are painted
glasse: over this roome are flatt Leads from whence you
enjoy the prospect of ye Garden &c. This building is of
Brick and is a gracefull Tower to your view of the Garden:
Now as you goe... from this gaye Paradise into the
darksome, deep Vault... where the Well is, it affects one
with a kind of Religious horrour. Round about the Well,
are fine potts of choice Plants. Of the earth that was digged
up for the making of this deep-walke & Grotto, was made
the Terrace, that reaches West & east, above it: from
where you might overlook the Garden. At each end of this
Terrace is a neat House to sitt and retire.[11]

It was in the idyllic setting of this garden that Herbert spent
much of his time when not at Cambridge or Westminster. In this
garden, Sir Francis Bacon, John Donne and John Aubrey were all
frequent visitors, walking along the gravel paths or playing bowls.
Indeed, metaphors and images from the game of bowls occur
frequently in Herbert's poetry. It was also, perhaps, where John
Danvers was happiest, for he was to become an increasingly
troubled and bitter soul as the years went by. John Aubrey
describes him walking in his garden in the summer mornings and
brushing his beaver hat on the hyssop and thyme, 'which did
perfume it with its naturall Spirit; and would last a morning or
longer'.[12]

'LAW SUTES CONSUME TIME, AND MONY, AND REST, AND
FRIENDS.'
Outlandish Proverbs No.776

The Virginia Company

The seeds of Sir John's bitterness can, perhaps, be found in his
dealings with the Virginia Company.

The first attempts to found a colony in Virginia had been the
work of Sir Walter Raleigh in the 1580s. The first colony ended in
failure—the colonists lasted a year, but had to be brought home by

Drake. Two years later 150 people set out to colonise the area and completely disappeared; probably they were massacred by the Indians. The protracted war with Spain prevented any further expeditions until 1604. In April 1606 the Government made the venture official, setting up the Royal Council for Virginia, with the express purpose of colonising America between the 34° and 45° latitudes.

Five hundred new colonists set out in 1607 under Captain Christopher Newport. They established the first permanent British colony in 1609 and called it Jamestown. They could hardly have chosen a worse site for their town: a low-lying marshy area. Malaria spread like wild-fire among the colony and soon food supplies were running short. In London, the Council realised that the enterprise was failing and would need drastic reorganisation and new finances. Accordingly, by Royal Assent, a new charter was drawn up in May 1609, by which the enterprise was given a commercial basis. The Virginia Company was formed.[13]

This gave the responsibility for directing the colony into the hands of the Company. Investors joined the Company either by purchasing shares of £12 10s. each or by emigrating—emigration counting as one share. The London company was made up of some 650 people, including 21 peers, 96 knights and more than 50 Members of Parliament. It was, therefore, an influential and powerful group and working for the Company was always seen as a desirable and honourable position. In 1609 John Donne made a futile attempt to become the Company Secretary. Although this attempt failed, his association continued. Some years later he would preach the annual sermon, and when he was Dean of St Pauls he was made an honorary member of the Council.[14]

The first task was to send some more people to the beleaguered colony. Accordingly, on 1 June 1609 an expedition of more than 500 emigrants sailed to Virginia. When they eventually arrived they found an appalling state of affairs. Disease and famine had ravaged the inhabitants of Jamestown, and of the 500 emigrants who had arrived the previous autumn only 60 were left. One man had even been executed for killing and eating his wife.[15]

Eventually a new settlement was established, on a higher site, called Henrico in honour of the young Prince of Wales. A succession of strict and efficient governors, starting with Lord Delawarr, enforced order on the settlements and began to achieve

results. Serious cultivation took place; treaties were concluded
with the local natives and a system of land tenantry was introduced. Among the staple crops which the settlers began to culti-
vate was tobacco.[16]

By this time Nicholas Ferrar, Herbert's acquaintance from
Cambridge, was heavily involved in the Company. He had taken
over from his father who had bequeathed to the company the sum
of £300 to build a college for educating the native children in the
Christian religion. This missionary side of the enterprise was
attractive to many investors, and from the start it was seen as an
opportunity for spreading the gospel.[17]

It may have been this Christian zeal, as much as the family
links, that interested Herbert in the Company. In later life he was
to eulogise the challenges and opportunities offered to 'the young
Gallant' by the Colonies, 'Where can he busie himself better, than
in those new Plantations, and discoveryes, which are not only a
noble, but also as they may be handled, a religious imployment?'[18] We must not, however, claim too much philanthropy or
religious zeal for the investors. First and foremost, the Virginia
Company was a commercial enterprise. It is difficult to believe
that Sir John Danvers, who had no particular reputation for
personal piety, would have been so involved in a mere missionary
enterprise.

We cannot be certain of what made the King decide to inter-
fere with the running of the Company. Much blame has been
levelled at Gondomar, the Spanish ambassador. Spain was wary
of increasing British power in the Americas, which she saw as
very much her own territory. At the same time, Charles was
fermenting his harebrained scheme of a Spanish alliance. Virgi-
nian tobacco was beginning to challenge the Spanish dominance
of this market. James actively disliked tobacco and regarded it as
an evil drug.

Perhaps the most important factor was James' exalted view of
the divine right of Kings. James held as an article of faith the fact
that he had been raised by God to govern Britain. The rule of the
monarchy was the divinely ordained means of government–and
yet here was a colony run by an elected official, which appeared to
be flourishing. Small wonder that the King looked on the new
political system with suspicion.

Certainly no love was lost between the King and the Company

Treasurer, Sir Edwyn Sandys, who harboured what James regarded as left-wing opinions. Thus it was that, at the quarterly meeting of the Company, held at Ferrar's house, a messenger arrived and indicated that the court should elect as their treasurer one of four men nominated by James, and no other. 'Choose the devil if you will,' James had said, 'but not Sir Edwyn Sandys.'[19]

By the next meeting the following June, a compromise had been reached. The King agreed that they could choose whom they liked, as long as it was someone who might at all times have access to the royal person. Sandys stood down, and, with great enthusiasm, the Company elected the Earl of Southampton—Shakespeare's patron—as their Treasurer.

However, the Royal interference was a warning sign that the King was preparing to take over the Company himself. Despite this amicable solution to the first clash, it could never end that way. One or other was always going to be defeated. And the disaster that befell the colony in 1622 ensured that it was the Company that lost. For on that day, the native tribes suddenly and without warning attacked the colony and slaughtered most of the inhabitants. In a few hours, over 350 people were butchered.[20]

After this disaster the Company was never the same again. When news reached England in June 1622, the company was immediately split by arguments and recriminations. In a fine display of shutting the stable door after the horse has bolted, a shipment of arms was dispatched to the colony. In May 1622, just before the storm broke, Nicholas Ferrar succeeded his brother John in the post of Deputy Treasurer. It was a post he was to fill admirably, keeping his nerve in the face of intense pressure.

James commissioned a propagandist to write an aggressive pamphlet, *The Unmasked Face of Our Colony in Virginia* and followed this up by indicting the Company in the Privy Council. Ferrar and Sandys managed to prepare a 5,000-word defence in only four days and the case was thrown out, but the pressure remained. The Earl of Southampton was told by a Privy Council member that their defence would 'avail nothing, for it is already determined that your patent is to be taken away and the Company dissolved'.[21]

The King set up a Royal Commission and, eventually, declared that the Company's charter would be revoked and that the colony would henceforth be run by a governor and twelve Councillors appointed by the Privy Council. Ferrar, realising that the minute books of the Company would be seized, embarked upon the massive job of preparing a copy of the previous five years' records. He worked with six clerks, finally finishing the task in June 1624. The Company may have been defeated, but the records would remain. In the end it proved a wise move, since all the records that James seized were conveniently 'lost'. Only the copy remains.[22]

When Parliament met in 1624, therefore, the Virginia Company was on everyone's lips. On 28 April 1624, Sir John Danvers and Nicholas Ferrar were among a group of Company members who presented their case to a committee of the House of Commons.[23] Parliament presented their petition to the King, asking him to confirm the privileges of the Company, but the House was peremptorily instructed that the affairs of the Company were now strictly under the control of King and Crown.

In the end, Parliament managed to extract something of a revenge by impeaching the Earl of Middlesex, the Lord Treasurer, on charges of bribery and corruption. Middlesex had been an opponent of the Company, active in trying 'to take the Patent from the Company, under the pretence, that it should be, & yeild to the King a greater Revenew than it did.'[24] Ferrar was actively involved in the impeachment–he spoke for the prosecution. The Earl was heavily fined and imprisoned in the Tower. For Ferrar, it was an unsatisfactory victory. Ever after, he worried that he had acted out of revenge and personal malice.

Despite the failure of Ferrar to secure the safety of the Virginia Company, he came out of the wreckage with a high personal reputation. He was offered government posts–Clerk to the Privy Council and Ambassador to Savoy–which he refused. He had decided that God was calling him to a life of seclusion. He set about setting up a religious community, the community that was to become Little Gidding.

It is difficult not to believe that Ferrar's example had an immense impact on Herbert. Here was a man of talents, a man of personal integrity and deep religious faith, who had chosen to eschew glory and personal honour. If Herbert had lost faith in the King–and the King's opposition to the missionary spirit of the

Virginia Company must have seemed proof positive of the monarch's decline–then Ferrar showed him an alternative way.

Early accounts play down the relationship between the two
men, despite the fact that the earliest account of Herbert's life–
the 1633 preface to *The Temple*–was written by Ferrar himself.
We owe our traditional impression of their friendship to Barnabas
Oley, who wrote the first substantial memoir of Herbert as a
preface to Herbert's *Remains* in 1652:

> There is another thing (some will call it a Paradox) which I
> learned from Him (and *Mr. Ferrer*) in the *Managery* of their
> most cordiall and *Christian Friendship*. That this may be
> maintained in vigour and height without the Ceremonies of
> Visits and Complements; yea without any Trade of secular
> courtesies, meerly in order to spirituall Edification of one
> another in love. I know they loved each other most
> entirely, and their very souls cleaved together most
> intimately, and drove a large stock of Christian Intelligence
> together long before their deaths: yet saw they not each
> other in many years, I think, scarce ever, but as Members
> of one Universitie, in their whole lives.[25]

It is to this tale of Oley that Walton owes his comment that
their 'holy friendship was long maintain'd without any interview,
but only by loving and endearing Letters'.[26]

Neither Walton nor Oley knew of the service of the two men in
the Parliament of 1624. Although Herbert was not as actively
concerned with the affairs of the Virginia Company as some
biographers would have us believe, given Sir John's involvement
in the affairs of the company, it would have been extremely
unlikely that George and Nicholas failed to renew the acquaintance they had struck up at Cambridge.

Herbert's duties in the Parliament of 1624 were not onerous.
He sat on only one committee–a committee appointed to investi-
gate accusations against teachers and academics. One of the tutors
they investigated (on unspecified charges) was John Richardson,
the master of George's own college, Trinity. Another was a
schoolmaster accused of popery.[27]

It was to prove Herbert's only experience of Parliament.
Despite its failure to save the Virginia Company, he was to
recommend the experience in *The Country Parson*:

> When there is a Parliament, he is to endeavour by all
> means to be a Knight or Burgess there; for there is no
> school to a Parliament. And when he is there, he must not
> only be a morning man, but at Committees also; for there
> the particulars are exactly discussed, which are brought
> from thence to the House but in generall.[28]

Parliament was prorogued–that is, its meetings were discontinued without dissolving Parliament itself–on May 29. Two weeks later on 11 June, Herbert was granted a Grace from the University allowing him a six-month leave of absence 'on account of many businesses away'.[29]

We cannot be sure what these 'many businesses' were. Perhaps Herbert intended to sit in the next sessions of Parliament in 1625. Although his name is printed as burgess for Montgomery in the Parliament of 1625, his name may well have been included by default. For in the following year there is no firm evidence that he attended any of the sessions.[30] If there was anything that the school of Parliament had taught Herbert, then it appears to have been that Westminster held no future for him.

12

1624-1626

Kent, Chelsea

'THOUGH YOU SEE A CHURCH-MAN ILL, YET CONTINUE IN
THE CHURCH STILL.'
Outlandish Proverbs No.698

Herbert's Ordination as Deacon

On 3 November 1624, the Archbishop of Canterbury granted a
special dispensation allowing Herbert to be ordained deacon by
John Williams, Bishop of Lincoln. The dispensation allowed
Williams to ordain Herbert at any time, without having to obtain
the usual letter of permission from his own bishop.[1]

The normal procedure for anyone wanting to be ordained
deacon would be for the candidate to announce his intention, and
then wait a year. It was also normal procedure for the ordinand to
be ordained by his own bishop. Had it just been a question of
Herbert wanting to be ordained by Williams, then his own bishop
could have given permission. Apparently, Herbert needed to be
ordained as soon as possible.

For Charles to argue that for Herbert to become deacon meant
'setting aside opportunity for secular advancement' is quite
wrong.[2] Andrewes was both a bishop and a member of the Privy
Council.[3] If he needed a further example, Herbert had to look no
further than the clergyman given permission to ordain him. John
Williams was by this time not only Dean of Westminster and
Bishop of Lincoln, but also Lord Keeper. Not that Herbert
would necessarily have had in mind to follow Williams' somewhat
unscrupulous example, but at least we need not infer that Herbert
had taken a decision to enter fully the parochial life. As Alan
Maycock has written:

> At that time...there was a sharper line than there is
> nowadays between diaconate and priesthood. The idea of
> the former as preparation for the latter is comparatively
> modern...Many men entered the diaconate without any
> intention of becoming Priests; and that tradition endured
> until at least the end of the seventeenth century.[4]

Indeed, Ferrar himself was only ever a deacon. If this initial step was taken because Herbert had finally decided to become a priest, we may reasonably ask why he waited for a further six years before doing so.

In which case, why the urgency? The most obvious reason was that Herbert was merely obeying college statutes. The Trinity College statute required all fellows to take orders within seven years. Herbert had missed this in 1623, but may well have been making up, as quickly as he could, for his omission. Whatever he felt about the university post, he was at this time backed into a corner. Even if the Orator's job had lost its savour, it was at least certain. Becoming a deacon was simply a case of obeying the university statutes.

We do not know the exact date of Herbert's ordination as deacon, but given the trouble taken to obtain the special dispensation, it probably took place before the end of 1624. He may have been ordained at the same time that Williams presented him with a portion of the church rectory at Llandinam, Montgomeryshire. The presentation, which took place on 6 December 1624, meant that Herbert was one of two men holding the rectory and therefore receiving a share of the tithes. He need not have been ordained deacon to be comportioner, but it seems likely that the two events occurred around the same time, and Herbert was to hold the post for the rest of his life. Whatever the case, his acceptance of this sinecure signals no serious intent to enter the ministry, for he never went near the church. He was exactly the same as the string of clerics who held the church in the seventeenth century, 'who never had the slightest intention of putting in residence in the Uplands of the Upper Severn'.[5]

'OF A NEW PRINCE, NEW BONDAGE.'
Jacula Prudentum No.1116

Death of King James

James died in 1625. Lying in his favourite hunting lodge at
Theobalds in Essex, attended by his son and the faithful 'Steenie',
he died in a haze of senility accelerated by a stroke.[6] Bishop
Williams administered the last rites and also preached at the
somewhat chaotic funeral two weeks later.

From the start, the reign of Charles I bore an ominous
resemblance to that of his father. The summer of 1624 had been
extremely dry followed by a mild and humid winter. February
had seen a series of high tides and the Thames had burst its
banks. A month later, as the King lay dying, the first outbreaks
of plague were reported in St Botolph-without-Bishopgate,
London.[7]

As before, Londoners fled the streets. According to Dekker,
for every 1,000 who died, five times that number had fled the
capital. In the plague of 1625 over 35,000 people–around one-
sixth of the population of the capital–died. It was the speed with
which the plague struck that was so terrifying. At a service of
deliverance held in August, three of the four officiating priests fell
mortally ill. People dropped dead in the streets.[8]

'AN OLD FRIEND, A NEW HOUSE.'
Outlandish Proverbs No.400

Herbert in Kent

Walton claims that, with James' death, Herbert's 'court-hopes'
also died and he retreated from London. As we have seen, he
effectively killed off his court-hopes some years earlier. It was
not, therefore, the death of his court-hopes, but the outbreak of
the pestilence, which caused Herbert to 'Retreat from *London*, to
a friend in *Kent*'.[9] Here, newly ordained as deacon, he 'liv'd very
privately, and was such a lover of solitariness, as was judg'd to
impair his health, more than his Study had done.' For Herbert it
was a time of deep thinking and reassessment.

It was to this period that Walton assigned Herbert's decision to be ordained. 'In this time of Retirement, he had many Conflicts with himself, Whether he should return to the painted pleasures of a Court-life, or betake himself to a study of Divinity, and enter into Sacred Orders?'[10]

Although Walton is painting a fanciful picture, it is true to say that for the next five years, Herbert found it extremely difficult to come to any decision. He had seen at first hand the machinations of power and had turned away. He had rejected court, he had rejected university, he had rejected Parliament. What was there left?

It is entirely possible that his ordination, taken hurriedly and to fulfil university statutes, became the only option that Herbert found at all palatable. During this period in Kent he no doubt considered his position, and began to see the way in which God had led his life.

We have already noted how Herbert referred to illness as punishment, but this is just one part of the way in which he viewed the world. As Rosemond Tuve points out, Herbert saw the world as 'a web of significancies not as a collection of phenomena which we may either endow with significance or leave unendowed...'[11]

That God had given him his gifts he was never in doubt. But if God had given him the gifts, he had frequently taken away the opportunities for using them. It is interesting to note how often when Herbert talks about taking Orders or following God, that he talks of lack of choice. Rarely does he scale the heights in 'The Pearl', where he knowingly rejects the ways of learning, honour and pleasure; 'I flie to thee, and fully understand/Both the main sale, and the commodities;/And at what rate and price I have thy love'.[12] Far more frequently, Herbert's God is a loving God, but also a God who 'betrays',[13] who 'cross-biases' his child, 'taking me from my way'.[14] God has 'hunted' him down,[15] laid 'Fine nets and strategems to catch us in'.[16] Herbert was eventually to come to accept God's will and more, to find the security and peace he had always yearned for, but throughout his poetry he talks of God as the one who takes away his choices, who thwarts his plans:

> But that thou art my wisdome, Lord,
>   And both mine eyes are thine,

My minde would be extreamly stirr'd
   For missing my designe.

Were it not better to bestow
   Some place and power on me?
Then should thy praises with me grow,
   And share in my degree.
                        Submission[17]

The idea that Herbert was, from the start, determined on becoming a priest is not borne out by his poetry. His 'designe' was always to marry heaven and earth in secular preferment. Even once he had taken the decision to enter the priesthood, the ghosts of his past desires would not let him go;

But when I view abroad both Regiments;
               The worlds, and thine:
Thine clad with simplenesse, and sad events;
               The other fine,
   Full of glorie and gay weeds,
   Brave language, braver deeds:
That which was dust before, doth quickly rise,
               And prick mine eyes.
                        Frailtie[18]

This is hardly the language of the ecstatic convert. Of course, we must tread carefully here. Critics have rightly pointed out the danger of taking Herbert's poems as purely autobiographical. His poetry, it is true, cannot be 'confined within the category of spiritual autobiography'.[19] But it cannot be denied that his poems are to some degree expressions of personal faith. Even when Herbert is dealing with Old Testament types and symbols, those symbols had a personal relevance for him. He, after all, selected them.

A poem such as 'Joseph's Coat', for example, works on several levels. At one level it refers to the story of Joseph as found in Genesis. At another level, Joseph's coat was a commonplace 'type' for Christ; pictures of Christ's crucifixion were often accompanied in medieval manuscripts by drawings of Jacob being shown the bloodied coat of his son. And at yet another level, the poem is clearly about Herbert himself. For Joseph's story was also George's:

> Wounded I sing, tormented I indite,
> Thrown down I fall into a bed, and rest:
> Sorrow hath chang'd its note: such is his will,
> Who changeth all things, as him pleaseth best.[20]

Perhaps the best example is the verse which, according to Ferrar, was Herbert's 'own Motto, with which he used to conclude all things that might seem to tend any way to his own honour'. The verse was, *'Lesser then the least of Gods mercies.'*[21] The phrase, which is also the refrain of Herbert's poem, 'The Posie', is derived from Genesis 32:10, where Jacob is renamed Israel: 'I am not worthy of the least of all the mercies and all the truth, which thou hast shewed unto thy servant.' The context of the verse, though, would have been apparent to any contemporary readers of Herbert, steeped as they were in the Bible. For Jacob wrestled with God. He lost the fight and was wounded in the struggle, yet the defeat led him into a time of great blessing and fulfilment. Herbert was not passively aware of these parallels; the parallels were the reason why the verse was so important to him.

It was in these wilderness years that Herbert wrestled with God. Over the years he came to accept and even embrace God's plan for him. But, like Jacob, he was wounded in the process.

'WE MUST RECOILE A LITTLE, TO THE END WE MAY LEAP
THE BETTER.'
Jacula Prudentum No.1121

Herbert and Donne

No doubt the thoughts that filled Herbert's mind during his stay in Kent were further developed by his retreat at his mother's house in Chelsea. There in 1625-26 he sheltered from the plague, along with an old friend of the family, John Donne.

In a letter dated 21 December 1625 Donne wrote to Sir Henry Goodyer, 'Mr. *George Herbert* is here.'[22] Donne's example demonstrated to Herbert that not only was the priesthood a noble calling, but that a man of abilities could still gain prominence even within the 'simplenesse, and sad events' of the church.

The relationship between George Herbert and John Donne is, like so many of Herbert's associations, a little hazy. On his ordination in 1615, Donne sent a poem to Herbert, in a letter sealed with his new seal; and towards the end of his life, Donne sent his friend the same seal on a ring. The seal – a figure of Christ crucified on an anchor, the symbol of hope – inspired Herbert to send a Latin poem in return.[23] At the time of their meeting in 'Chelsey', Donne had been a close friend of Magdalene Herbert for at least fifteen years, possibly even twenty-five. He would therefore have known Herbert well and followed his career. One can easily imagine them strolling along the gravel paths of Sir John's famous garden, or playing bowls on the green. Perhaps the Dean of St Paul's extolled the virtues of the religious life, to which he, too, had been forced to turn.

Nevertheless, even if Herbert had been persuaded to follow the example of Nick Ferrar and consecrate himself to God's service, there were difficulties. Ferrar had a private income; Herbert had a constant struggle for money. Ferrar had the support of his family; Herbert was dogged by illness, by parental opposition, by lack of funds and by the indecisiveness that formed part of his character.

'GREAT FORTUNE BRINGS WITH IT GREAT MISFORTUNE.'
Jacula Prudentum No.1144

Last Activities in Cambridge

The Grace given by the Cambridge Senate allowed Herbert only a six month leave of absence, but there are no indications that he was much evident at Cambridge any time after the summer of 1624. If Herbert had not exactly given up his university life, he never again took much interest in it. Herbert did not deliver the oration on the death of James I, which would have been a chance to repair the breach between himself and the new king, Charles. Instead, his deputy Herbert Thorndike made the oration at Great St Mary's.

He performed one last oration, however, on the installation of Buckingham as Lord Chancellor of the university in July 1626.

The text of this has been lost, but there is no doubt that Herbert delivered the official speech. It would be interesting to see how he managed to compliment a man who had only been elected by a majority of three votes, and even that unimpressive result had been the result of ballot-rigging.[24] Buckingham was in the midst of an impeachment trial at the time. Whether Charles intended Buckingham's election to be a slap in the face of Parliament, or whether he was merely concerned with tightening up university discipline, the House of Commons demanded an enquiry into the election, but Charles, whose handling of Parliament made his father look like a master of diplomacy by comparison, ordered the members to cease the investigation. When they did so he sent them a crowing letter.[25] Whatever Herbert said, to attempt to get into Buckingham's good books at this stage would have been futile, for George's cousin Edward had been one of the members of Parliament who had spoken out for the Duke's impeachment, arguing that he held too many high positions and that he had bribed his way into the office of Admiral and Lord Warden of the Cinque Ports. Even though Buckingham's royal protection meant that the impeachment was bound to fail, he would not have been disposed to look kindly on the relative of one who had accused him.[26]

After that Herbert had, effectively, left the university. His only other contact with it was not the official paying of compliments, but an obligation to an old friend.

Herbert had long been associated with Francis Bacon, Lord Verulam. He may have made Bacon's acquaintance through Sir John Danvers, with whom Bacon was friendly, or he may have met the great man, when Bacon feasted the entire university at Christmas 1613.[27] Whatever the case, the friendship had ripened over the years. Herbert had not only written to Bacon officially at least twice; he had exchanged poems, he had helped to translate Bacon's *The Advancement of Learning* and in 1625 Bacon dedicated his *Translation of Certaine Psalmes into English* to his 'very good friend, Mr. George Herbert'.[28]

By 1624, Bacon's star had fallen from the skies. This 'Prince of Theories and High priest of Truth' had been impeached, fined and disgraced.[29] There is, as Hutchinson says, something chivalrous about the rôle Herbert played in helping to organise the commemorative volume of verses on the occasion of Bacon's

death in 1626. The university, with typical regard for its own
safety, kept a safe distance from this tribute to the ruined states-
man, even to the extent of ensuring the book was printed in
London. The volume included verses from ten members of Trinity College, seven of them ex-Westminster students.[30] Herbert's
contribution was a poem which praised Bacon for his eloquence.[31]

Walton says that at this time he kept his links with Cambridge
only at the urging of his mother.

> But his Mother would by no means allow him to leave the
> University, or to travel; and, though he inclin'd very much
> to both, yet he would by no means satisfie his own desires
> at so dear a rate, as to prove an undutiful Son to so
> affectionate a Mother; but did always submit to her
> wisdom.[32]

Yet, according to Walton, 'his dear Mother had often persuaded him' to take orders. Perhaps she wanted the best of both
worlds, to 'both eat thy cake and have it'.[33] Her piety and
religious sensibility would have appreciated and encouraged Herbert's hesitant desire to serve his God, and perhaps that is why
she often urged him to take orders, but at the same time she was
aware of the honour and security offered by the Oratorship.

So Herbert remained in a peculiar limbo of indecision. He was
still University Orator, yet he no longer visited the university. He
had half stepped into the world of the clergy, but was that what he
really wanted? He had made a decision of a sort, but still he
seemed to be drifting. If God had, indeed, caught him in his net,
then he was still a long way from being hauled in.

13

1626

Woodford, Leighton Bromswold

'HEE THAT GETS OUT OF DEBT, GROWES RICH.'
Outlandish Proverbs No.9

Henry Herbert

Some time in the summer of 1625, Sir Henry Herbert married Susan Slyford Plomer, widow of Edmund Plomer, merchant tailor.

Sir Henry's life had, up until this point, been the most successful of all the Herbert brothers. 'After he had been brought up in Learning,' wrote Edward, 'as the other brothers were, [Henry] was sent by his Friends into France, where he attained the Language of that Country in much perfection.'[1] Henry first travelled to France in 1615, where he did more than just practise his pronunciation: he acted as an official courier. In August 1615 he was arrested in Boulogne while on official business and was held prisoner until September. Despite this mishap he continued to act as a courier and later spent time in France as a confidential secretary to his brother, during Edward's ill-fated spell as ambassador.[2]

He was at court in 1622, then served under the Sydney family at Goude, fighting on the side of the Prince of Orange during the interminable wars in the Low Countries. On August 7 1623 James knighted him, when Henry was staying with Sir William Herbert, Earl of Pembroke at Wilton. Pembroke was a distant kinsman of Henry, George and the family, and at that time was Lord Chancellor. At the same time, according to Henry, the King 'was pleased likewise to bestowe many good words upon mee, and to receive mee as Master of the Revells.'[3]

As Master of the Revels, it was Henry's duty to license all the plays and entertainments that went on in the country. He was entitled to income gained from fees for the rights to perform, licensing of individual plays, and even licences granted to travelling showmen and players. (His first licensed performances were exhibitions of elephants, dromedaries, and–rather unexcitingly–beavers.) His charges were generally forty shillings for a new play and half that for a revival. He maintained that the fee was for the time he had to spend reading and judging the work and not for the licence–a distinction which meant that he still got paid even if the work was consigned to the fire. Henry was 'vitally interested in money-getting' and managed his business very astutely. As the years went by, he became remarkably skilled in the art of getting money out of the entertainment industry. He would have made a marvellous agent.[4]

Unlike his brothers, therefore, Henry succeeded at court. Although, like all the family, Henry sometimes found his oldest brother 'overbearing or difficult', Edward was always proud of Henry, signing his letters 'your faithful loving brother'.[5] Of all his brothers, Henry's marriage is the only one Edward mentions, probably because it was so signally different from his own. 'He came to Court, and was made Gentleman of the Kings privy Chamber, and Master of the Revells, by which means as also by a good Marriage, he attained to great fortunes, for himself and Posterity to injoy: he also hath given several proofs of his Courage in Duells...'[6]

Susan's husband had died the previous year, leaving her a very rich woman. She brought to the marriage a dowry of £5,000 and considerable estates at Woodford and Kilbourn in Essex. Henry's marriage, unlike Edward's, brought him wealth and prosperity.[7]

In 1626 Herbert came to stay with his brother at Woodford. From now until George entered into the living at Bemerton, he was to have no permanent base. Instead he moved from friend's house to friend's house, such as Dauntsey House, the home of Earl Danby the brother of Sir John Danvers; the home of his friend in Kent; and, of course, Henry's house in Woodford.[8]

Walton records George as visiting his brother in 1629, but, as Leishman has suggested, it is probable that the last numeral has been inverted and 1626 is a better date. Perhaps George was present as a proud uncle when Susan Herbert gave birth to their first son, William, born on 1 May 1626. It may well be that at

Woodford Herbert organised the collection of materials for the
Francis Bacon memorial volume.

George was always close to Henry. When they were young, in
the Charing Cross house, they had shared a private tutor. They
both had a passion for proverbs—silly, or 'outlandish' sayings
which they swapped like stamps. After his death, two of George's
collections of proverbs were published.

'BUILDING IS A SWEET IMPOVERISHING.'
Outlandish Proverbs No.459

Leighton Bromswold

On 5 July 1626, Herbert was installed as a canon of Lincoln
Cathedral and prebendary of Leighton Ecclesia.[9] He did not
attend the service and was installed by proxy, one Peter Walker
standing in for him.[10] The 'corps of the prebend', in Oley's
words, was the church of Leighton Bromswold near Huntingdon.
It was not necessary for the prebend to live anywhere near the
church, since the parish was covered by a vicar. Neither were the
responsibilities of the office onerous, comprising mainly of
preaching an annual sermon in Lincoln Cathedral every Whitsunday, and reciting Psalms 31 and 32 in private every day. There
were also some charges that Herbert incurred for the services of
various officials in the cathedral. Even the preaching of the annual
Pentecost sermon was optional, since he could always choose to
pay ten shillings for a deputy to stand in.[11]

Again one is faced by the quandary. If Herbert was so keen to
embrace the cloth, why was he not there to be installed in person?
Why did he choose instead to attend in July 1626 the installation
of Buckingham as Chancellor of the University of Cambridge?
Was this some last desperate throw of the dice, a last attempt to
curry favour?

In truth, the post seems to have been little more than a sinecure. He was already comportioner at Llandinam, which
brought him in some money; the presentation of Leighton Bromswold would add to his purse, albeit not greatly. It was not until
three years later, when he had once and for all decided on the
priesthood, that we have any record of Herbert actually fulfilling
his duties—he is listed in a preaching list of 1629 as having

preached the required sermon.[12] However, it is likely that he
visited the region more than once. Though the induction at the
cathedral, for example, could be undertaken by proxy, it was
usually expected that the new prebend would be inducted in
person into the living, on the spot, as it were. So it is probable
that Herbert did travel north at least one other time to be inducted in person at Leighton Bromswold.[13]

If he did, he would have been presented with an unprepossessing sight.

> This *Layton Ecclesia* [wrote Walton] is a Village near to
> *Spalden* in the County of *Huntington*, and the greatest part
> of the Parish Church was fallen down, and that of it which
> stood, was so decayed, so little, and so useless, that the
> Parish-Parishioners could not meet to perform their Duty
> to God in publick prayer and praises; and thus it had been
> for almost 20 years, in which time there had been some
> faint endeavours for a publick Collection, to enable the
> Parishioners to rebuild it, but with no success...[14]

When Herbert became prebend, therefore, the church was
unfit for public worship. Services had been held in the nearby
manor hall of the Duke of Lennox.[15] The dereliction of the
church makes it all the more likely that Herbert viewed the
position as a sinecure. If he had really meant this as his first
serious step into the priesthood, he would hardly have chosen a
derelict church. Such a well-connected person as Herbert would
at least have obtained a church that was capable of being used.

He did at least decide to rebuild the church. Perhaps it was
guilt that motivated him. Or perhaps it was the first time he
realised fully the importance of the church for the local community. If he was not prepared to enter fully into the life of the
church, he was at least ready to pull all the strings he could to
help them rebuild. John Ferrar, Nicholas's brother, who later
took a major part in the restoration project, estimated that the
church restoration would cost 'at the least upon two thousand
pounds'.[16] Whatever motivated Herbert, however, his initial
fund-raising efforts do not appear to have borne much fruit, for
no serious work began at Leighton until summer 1632.[17] In the
end, Herbert was to leave much of the supervision work in the

hands of the Ferrars, and much of the fund-raising in the hands of his brother Henry.

If he did visit Leighton, he could also have stayed with Nicholas Ferrar, whose community of Little Gidding was nearby. Perhaps Ferrar would even have attended the service of induction itself, along with Maurice Hughes, the vicar at Leighton. It seems reasonable to suppose that he visited Little Gidding at least once and saw what went on there. Herbert certainly corresponded frequently with the community at Little Gidding, even sending Ferrar the manuscript of his poems from his deathbed. It is inconceivable that they did not meet at least once in the last eight years of Herbert's life. It is likely that they met, albeit infrequently, either when Ferrar's business took him to London, or when Herbert made one of his rare trips north to Lincolnshire.

'HE THINKES NOT WELL, THAT THINKES NOT AGAINE.'
Outlandish Proverbs No.836

Indecision

Gradually, Herbert was coming to accept that he should be ordained priest. Whilst Leighton Bromswold was merely a sinecure, he did at least accept the prebend and he did try to do something about the parlous state of the church. Yet still he held back from that final commitment.

Part of the problem was his own indecision. His poems refer to his wanting employment; 'All things are busie; onely I/ Neither bring hony with the bees,/ Nor flowres to make that, nor the husbandrie/ To water these.'[18] As long as he could not make up his mind one way or the other, he was withering away.

Evidently he did not feel what he thought he should feel. His breast did not swell with the presence of the Lord. On the contrary, he frequently felt 'as barren to thy praise/ As is the dust'[19] It was to be years before Herbert realised that to wait for the right feelings was futile; he would never 'feel' right or worthy enough to be a priest. But take the action, and the feelings would follow.

He may also have still been battling with feelings of honour and family pride. The exploits of his brother Henry may have made him feel, more keenly than ever, his failure to get on at court. Our pride is not hurt when we reject something, it is when we are the something rejected that it hurts. Even though Herbert had offended Charles, his subsequent actions show that he had not entirely given up hope. He was, however, a forgotten man.

'HEALTH AND MONY GOE FARRE.'
Outlandish Proverbs No.447

Illnesses

Another reason for his reluctance to commit himself was illness. He had been seriously ill again in the beginning of 1626, siezed by what Walton calls a 'sharp *Quotidian Ague*' which struck him during his '34th year'.[20] Seventeenth-century medicine defined three kinds of fever depending on the frequency of attacks. A quotidian fever was the most severe of the three, bringing an attack every day, which could be either mild or severe. Walton's 'sharp' indicates that the fever was acute. The patient's temperature would rise dangerously, and he would suffer increasingly violent paroxysms. Usually, such attacks were fatal.[21]

The Crosse, one of his most autobiographical poems, may well date from Herbert's time as prebend of Leighton Bromswold, although as it is not in *W*, it may equally date from a later period. If it does date from the time when he was involved in Leighton Bromswold, it is not for the reason that Amy Charles states: that the 'Crosse' which she says, 'almost certainly refers to the Church at Leighton Bromswold' since that was the only cruciform church with which Herbert was involved.[22] But the 'Crosse' in the title does not refer to the 'place' mentioned in line two. The 'Crosse' refers to Christ's words in Matthew, 'Then said Jesus unto his disciples, If any *man* will come after me, let him deny himself , and take up his cross and follow me.'[23]

The particular cross that Herbert had to bear was illness. Even when he had reached a decision, a point when he had found a place where he could 'sing and serve thee', God had taken away his power to do even that.

And then when after much delay,
        Much wrastling, many a combate, this deare end,

> So much desir'd is giv'n, to take away
> My power to serve thee; . . .[24]

Like Jacob, after 'much wrastling' he had been wounded in the struggle. It had been a fight between Herbert and God to get Herbert to submit to God's will. Now, God had 'touched him on the hip', taking away his physical power to perform the duties expected of him.

'I am in all a weak disabled thing' he wrote.[25] It was this that caused his mother – herself ill – to worry about his health.

> His mother being inform'd of his intentions to Re-build
> that Church: and apprehending the great trouble and
> charge that he was likely to draw upon himself, his
> Relations, and Friends, before it could be finisht; sent for
> him from *London* to *Chelsey* (where she then dwelt) and at
> his coming, said – '*George*, I sent for you, to perswade you
> to commit Simony, by giving your Patron as good a gift as
> he has given you; namely, that you give him back his
> Prebend: for, *George*, it is not for your weak body, and
> empty purse, to undertake to build Churches.'

George refused her request, asking her that for the first time in his life he would become 'an *undutiful Son*'.[26]

Although we have to take whatever Walton reports with a lorry load of salt, this exchange has the authentic feel of a mother's concern. Again there is this ambivalence in Magdalene. As soon as her son started taking his sinecure seriously, she wanted him to give back his gift. It is clear that pressure from his mother only added to his indecision. She it was who wanted him to continue as University Orator when all his actions show that he wished to relinquish it, perhaps as early as 1624. She was worried about his health, but there is also something almost parsimonious about her anxiety about the cost to Herbert's family and friends.

Which brings us to perhaps the main reason he was holding back from the final step: he had no money. While he was poor, he was dependent on his family. He had some income from Leighton Bromswold and some from Llandinam and his infrequently received £30 annuity from his brother, but that was all. Most of his income from the Orator's post went on paying people to do the job for him in his absence.

By the start of 1627, he was still in a state of limbo. Leighton Bromswold, if it was a serious step towards the priesthood, was only a tiny step. There were still too many things holding him back: he was plagued by the *Quotidian Ague*; he was, if not poor, then impecunious; he was trying to respect the wishes of his mother and he did not feel the joy in his heart that he was certain all priests felt.

The following year, all but one of these circumstances was to change.

CHAPTER

14

1626-1627

Woodford, Chelsea, Ribbesford

'A LITTLE WITH QUIET IS THE ONELY DYET.'
Outlandish Proverbs No.327

Illness and Cures

As we have seen, George came to his brother's house in the throes
of a serious illness. Like his days in Cambridge, Herbert 'thought
to remove it by the change of Air: to which end he went to
Woodford in Essex'. He remained at Woodford, on and off, for
about a year, and while he was there underwent a regime aimed to
cure his ague.

> In his [Henry's] House he remain'd about Twelve Months,
> and there became his own Physitian, and cur'd himself of
> his Ague, by forbearing Drink and not eating any Meat, no
> not Mutton, nor a Hen, or Pidgeon, unless they were
> salted; and by such a constant Dyet, he remov'd his
> Ague...[1]

The self-imposed cure was only partially successful. It certainly removed the ague, but 'with inconveniences that were
worse; for he brought upon himself a disposition to Rheums, and
other weaknesses, and a supposed Consumtion'.

Like all congenital invalids, Herbert was always fascinated by
cures. In *The Country Parson* he exhorts all parsons to be alert to
illness, 'if there be any of his flock sick, hee is their Physician'.[2]
To become acquainted with medical knowledge is, according to
Herbert, a simple enough exercise:

> Yet it is easie for any Scholer to attaine to such a measure

120

of Phisick, as may be of much use to him both for himself,
and others. This is done by seeing one Anatomy, reading
one Book of Phisick, having one Herball by him. And let
Fernelius be the Phisick Authour, for he writes briefly,
neatly, and judiciously...[3]

The Parson should also have a thorough knowledge of herbs
and their uses. 'And surely hyssope, valerian, mercury, adders
tongue, yerrow, melilot, and Saint *Johns* wort made into a salve;
And Elder, camomill, mallowes, comphrey and smallage made
into a Poultis have done great and rare cures.'[4]

At this time, Herbert was not only learning about the 'rare/
And curious vertues both of herbs and stones'[5] but may well have
been reading about the virtues of the strict diet in Lessius's Latin
translation of Luigi Cornaro's *Trattato de la vita sobria*. Herbert
was, either at this time or later, to translate this into English
under the title, *A Treatise of Temperance and Sobrietie*.

John Ferrar writing some thirty years later said that the
inspiration and guidance for the translation came from Nicholas
Ferrar.[6] In all probability, it was the opposite way around, for the
anonymous 'T.S.' who wrote a preface to *Hygiasticon* (1634) in
which the translation was first published, describes the English
publication:

> Master *George Herbert* of blessed memorie, having at the
> request of a Noble Personage translated it into English,
> sent a copie thereof, not many moneths before his death,
> unto some friends of his, who a good while before had
> given an attempt of regulating themselves in matter of
> Diet...[7]

The 'friends' were probably the community at Little Gidding.
Nicholas, in particular, would have been interested in this work;
when, as a young man, he was taken ill at Padua, he had been
advised that 'he was his own best physician' and that he should
'observe a regularity in his diet'.[8] It may be that the 'Noble
Person' who requested the English translation was Francis Bacon,
who referred to 'the regiment and Diet which the Venetian Cor-
narus used', in his *Historia Vitae et Mortis* of 1623. Given Bacon's
admiration for Herbert's linguistic abilities, it is altogether likely
that he recommended the book to Herbert's attention.

The parallels between the lives of author and translator would have appealed to Herbert's sense of symbolism. Cornaro, like Herbert, was 'affected from the thirtie fifth yeare of my age to the fortieth, having tried all remedies fruitlesly'. He therefore resolved to pursue a *'sober and orderly life'*, with dramatic effect: 'Upon this, I found within a few dayes, that I was exceedingly helped, and by continuance thereof, within lesse than one yeare (although it may seem to some incredible) I was perfectly cured of all my infirmities.'[9]

Although the cure was not to be so dramatic in Herbert's case, he began a devotion to fasting and temperance that was to last the rest of his life, particularly as a parson:

> The Parson in his house observes fasting dayes...which he celebrates not only with abstinence of diet, but also of company, recreation, and all outward contentments; and besides, with confession of sins, and all acts of Mortification. Now fasting dayes containe a treble obligation; first, of eating lesse that day, then on other dayes; secondly, of eating no pleasing, or over-nourishing things, as the Israelites did eat sowre herbs: Thirdly of eating no flesh...[10]

These were not, incidentally, sentiments that the rest of his family necessarily shared, for in the 1620s Sir John Danvers made regular payments to St Martins-in-the-Fields church of 14s.4d. for a licence allowing him to eat flesh in Lent.[11]

'PRAISE DAY AT NIGHT, AND LIFE AT THE END.'
Outlandish Proverbs No.97

Death of Magdalene Herbert

Herbert probably remained in Woodford until May 1627, when he was called to Chelsea where his mother was severely ill. As she had advanced into her sixties, as already noted, she had been subject to increasing illness and depression:

> And for her, some sicknesses in the declination of her yeeres, had opened her to an overflowing of *Melancholie*;

> Not that she ever lay under that *water*, but yet, had
> sometimes, some high Tides of it; and, though this
> distemper would sometimes cast a cloud, and some halfe-
> damps upon her naturall cheerfulnesse, and sociablenesse,
> and sometimes induce darke, and sad apprehensions...

Through it all she had remained convinced of 'God's proceedings'
and 'his mercy and goodness towards her and all hers'.[12]

She died in early June 1627.

If her death was a release from her infirmities, it was also, in a
way, a release for her son. He wrote a letter in May 1627, to
Robert Creighton, his Deputy Orator, which to all effect is a
Latin resignation letter. That he had remained Orator for so long
was at her behest; with her death, he no longer needed to remain
in such an anomalous position. He resigned, to be officially
succeeded by Creighton the following January.[13]

George was deeply attached to his mother. She had raised him,
educated him and supported him through the years. He had never
known a father—Sir John was more of an elder brother than
anything else. The true depth of Herbert's emotion can be found
in the verses he wrote immediately following her death. The
Memoriae Matris Sacrum were written in Latin and Greek and
show little of the fatuous display of his earlier Latin poetry:

> Now you see that the boundless beauty of her brilliant
>   face
> Was not perishable, was not of the body but of the
>   mind—
> Her mind that once through her body shone and now
>   through
> Heaven, as through a window, shines.[14]

Not that the overstatement of the professional orator was
entirely absent. Take the 'Epitaphium':

> Here lies the glory and victory of the feminine sex:
>   Chaste virgin, faithful wife, stern parent:
> The beloved prize of peer and commoner alike:
> She captivated the one with her nobility, the other with
>   her piety:

So exalted and humble at once, she join'd remote
        places:
She delighted in things earthly and things heavenly.[15]

The sequence consists of nineteen poems, thirteen in Latin,
then five in Greek, then a final Latin section. Magdalene Herbert
is celebrated as a warm, caring, able, witty woman:

No occasion could unnerve her,
And from the start she had it in her grip.
Ah, this very storm, this very grace of speech
Stern winsomeness, wit
And wisdom mixed.[16]

It is in the Greek poems, more than any other, that Herbert
escapes from the excesses so characteristic of his other classical
verse. The Greek sections are measured and eloquent, and full of
the impotent helplessness of grief:

It is difficult, I think, to shed tears,
And it is difficult not to shed tears;
But it is more difficult than anything
That they who are weeping take rest.[17]

If the conceits are sometimes laborious, they are pierced with
the passion of one who has lost his only parent:

I cry woe for my mother, and women cry woe again,
        who
Not now are being stricken to the heart with gratitude
        for her who is fallen,
But are being stabbed with sore grief; for when they
Are talking together about her, being unmindful of
Their embroidery lifted up on high, the needle pricks
        their heart with a perilous wound,
When they miss the mark of their work while fashioning
For my mother a new gown, stained with blood, similar
        in colour to lamentation and grief.[18]

At times, *Memoriae Matris Sacrum* gives us a revealing glimpse
into Herbert's recent life, perhaps at the house in Kent. He talks

of his life in the country, where he has been working in his garden:

> Out in the country
> I have a tiny house with a panelled ceiling
> Ten roof beams in it: I have
> A little garden too, where space
> Fights it out with flower's fleece; still it is
> The kind a tasteful owner wants...(Poem XIX).[19]

From there he has come to Chelsea, where he watches the 'White-capped waves of the Thames' (Poem XVIII).[20] He admits to neglecting his poetry, but if the death of his mother is the act of his Muse, anxious to get him writing again, then he rejects it; 'You drove me to it, and I write; but hearken, foolish Muse: this once I write, but not again.'[21] The death of his mother has taken away his guide, leaving him 'between weeping and danger on all sides'. 'To die,' he writes, 'is better to live without purpose.'[22]

Lady Danvers was buried in Chelsea in June. On 1 July, John Donne, the Dean of St Paul's, came to preach her memorial service. The service was, as we have seen, the only time that Izaak Walton saw George Herbert. having travelled to Chelsea to hear Donne preach. The sermon that Donne preached on that occasion was published a week later; and in the same volume, the series of poems that Herbert had written: *Memoriae Matris Sacrum; 'Sacred to the memory of his mother'*.

'SPEAKE NOT OF MY DEBTS, UNLESSE YOU MEAN TO PAY
THEM.'
Outlandish Proverbs No.998

The Manor of Ribbesford

The landscape of Herbert's life was changing. His mother, who had formed such a part of his life, was gone.

Two weeks after the publication of *Memoriae Matris Sacrum*, the Crown granted the manor of Ribbesford jointly to Edward and George Herbert and their cousin Thomas Lawley.[23] The manor seems to have been granted as a response to Edward's persistent claims for compensation for his ambassadorial

expenses, as well as a very minor recognition of the other relatives.[24] Later in the same year, they were able to turn this valuable
asset into cash, when the manor was purchased by Henry Herbert, using £3,000 of the £5,000 his wife had brought with her as a
dowry. For George, it was the end of years of subsisting on
handouts from his family and minor payments from his employment. At last he was financially independent.

He now moved. During 1627 and 1628, he had been living
between Chelsea and Woodford. Perhaps it was the change in his
step-father's life, and the ensuing turmoil at Chelsea, that caused
him to move. For on 10 July, 1628, a little over a year after the
death of his first wife, Sir John Danvers remarried. His new wife
Elizabeth Dauntsey brought with her the estate of Lavington in
Wiltshire, where Sir John immediately set about laying out formal and elaborate gardens.[25]

Initially, George went to Henry's newly acquired manor at
Ribbesford, just outside Bewdley in Worcestershire. His signa-
ture is on an indenture dated 14 July 1628, by which Sir Henry
settled the manor of Ribbesford on his wife if he should die before
her. George is recorded as 'George Herbert of Chelsey in the
County of Midd Esquire'.[26] It was probably a few months after
that, according to Walton, that he removed to 'Dantsey
[Dauntsey] in Wiltshire, a noble house which stands in a choice
Air.'

It was at some time during these years that Sir John appointed
Arthur Woodnoth to manage his business affairs, a job which
grew increasingly more difficult as the years went by. The failure
of the Virginia Company had soured Sir John's relations with the
King and court, and in the ensuing years he experienced more
and more financial difficulties, which, it was said, only served to
exacerbate his disloyal tendencies.[27] Perhaps the trigger for this
decline was the death of Magdalene Herbert. She had provided
the headstrong Sir John with a stability that later wives could
never match. The years after her death saw him engage on more
and more overspending on his houses and gardens, as if all the
extravagance that had been bottled up inside him had been let
loose. Although there is little documentary evidence, Herbert
probably continued to see his step-father, especially since he was
to become very close to Arthur Woodnoth, his business manager.
When Herbert died, Sir John was even appointed the overseer of

his will, which indicates that George, at least, still had faith in his step-father's business acumen.[28]

Another factor which kept George and Sir John in close contact was that George was now staying with Sir John's brother. The owner of Dauntsey House was Sir Henry Danvers, the Earl of Danby and the elder brother of Sir John. The Earl of Danby, 'lov'd Mr. Herbert very much' according to Walton.[29] They shared many interests, including gardens and gardening – Henry founded the Botanical Garden at Oxford. Dauntsey was a village near Chippenham in Wiltshire, surrounded by rolling countryside. Herbert had time for walking and riding. In this house, according to Walton, 'by a *spare Dyet*, declining all *perplexing studies*, moderate exercise, and a cheerful conversation, his health was apparently improv'd to a good degree of strength and chearfulness.'[30]

CHAPTER

15

1629

Wiltshire

'HEE LOOSETH NOTHING, THAT LOOSETH NOT GOD.'
Outlandish Proverbs No.35

The Year of Decisions

At the beginning of 1629, Herbert had been drifting for nearly five years. He had become a deacon, it is true, but he had failed to progress beyond that, through what can only have been his own decision. Now the time had come when he had to take decisions. The main obstacles in the way of his taking Holy Orders had been removed. Yet he was still adrift:

> I am no link of thy great chain,
> But all my companie is a weed.
> Lord, place me in thy consort; give one strain
> To my poore reed.
> 'Employment' (I)[1]

'Employment', with its strain of impotence, of being lost, perfectly sums up the aimlessness of Herbert during this period. He was still at Cambridge, yet he had left. He had taken one step into the priesthood, but his church, such as it was, was many miles away from him; and anyway, there is no evidence to show that he felt the inclination to go and serve God in his parish.

Some days he would feel as though God was calling him. Some days he would climb to the top of the mountain, only to plunge into the darkness the other side:

> It cannot be. Where is that mighty joy,
> Which just now took up all my heart?

> Lord, if thou must needs use thy dart,
> Save that, and me; or sin for both destroy.
> 'The Temper' (II)[2]

Indeed, this sense of moodiness and depression is a common theme of his poems:

> Although there were some fourtie heav'ns, or more,
> Sometimes I peere above them all;
> Sometimes I hardly reach a score,
> Sometimes to hell I fall.
> 'The Temper' (I)[3]

References to 'death' and 'dullness' are littered through his poems. 'My stock lies dead, and no increase/ Doth my dull husbandrie improve,'[4] he wrote. The praise of God–that feeling which he believed all priests should feel naturally–he found impossible to summon: 'To write a verse or two is all the praise,/ That I can raise.'[5]

His illness tormented him, but only insofar as it symbolised his own sin and state of mind: 'My thoughts are all a case of knives,/ Wounding my heart/ With scatter'd smart.'[6] Indeed, illness is seen throughout his poems as much a spiritual as a physical state. For example, in 'Easter-wings' he writes, 'My tender age in sorrow did beginne:/ And still with sicknesses and shame/ thou didst so punish sinne,/That I became/ most thinne.'[7]

Herbert was his own metaphor. The enduring strength of his verse is that, in the same way as he viewed history as 'a web of significancies', he was able to turn his own life into a symbol of the struggle that all Christians face: the struggle to submit one's own will to the will of God.

In his most autobiographical poem, 'Affliction', he traces the course of his life from his early idealism about the church and serving God, through his illness, to the death of those close to him:

> When I got health, thou took'st away my life,
>   And more, for my friends die:
> My mirth and edge was lost; a blunted knife
>   Was of more use then I.
> Thus thinne and lean without a fence or friend,
> I was blown through with ev'ry storm and winde.
>
> Whereas my birth and spirit rather took
>   The way that takes the towne;
> Thou didst betray me to a lingring book,
>   And wrap me in a gown.
> I was entangled in the world of strife,
> Before I had the power to change my life.
>   'Affliction' (I)[8]

In the four years from 1624 he had lost not only supporters like Bacon and the Duke of Hamilton, but 'friends' in the sense of 'kin' like his mother and two of his brothers. Eventually he was able to come to terms with the fact that it was not that God did not want him to be famous and honoured, it was that he himself did not want to take that route. Deep within Herbert he was always attracted to the priesthood, but he disliked the feeling that he had been forced to take that route. God had 'betrayed' him to his present position, harrying, almost taunting him with illness, grief and unhappiness:

> I took thy sweetned pill, till I came where
> I could not go away, nor persevere.
>   'Affliction' (I)[9]

And even in this state, God throws him into more sickness, 'lest perchance I should too happie be/ In my unhappinesse...I read and sigh and wish I were a tree/ for sure then I should grow.' The poem ends with acceptance, but it is hard. If he cannot love God now, in the midst of this unhappiness, then it were better that he did not love God at all.

That however, was surely the point. Herbert always did love God, even when he felt there was nothing to love God for. Of course it was not always that way. For one thing, there were the special times – the times when he soared above the fortieth

heaven. Nothing took him there more often than the music that
he had loved from early childhood:

> Sweetest of sweets, I thank you: when displeasure
> Did through my bodie wounde my minde,
> You took me thence, and in your house of pleasure
> A daintie lodging me assign'd.
>
> 'Church-musick'[10]

Then there were times when prayer left him almost breathless
with words, the verse rushing out of him in an ecstasy of metaphor, struggling to find the right image, to express the inexpress-
ible:

> Prayer the churches banquet, Angels age,
>   Gods breath in man returning to his birth,
>   The soul in paraphrase, heart in pilgrimage,
> The Christian plummet sounding heav'n and earth;
> Engine against th' Almightie, sinners towre,
>   Reversed thunder, Christ side-piercing spear,
>   The six daies world transposing in an houre,
> A kind of tune, which all things heare and fear.
>
> 'Prayer'[11]

The images flood the page, increasingly exotic. Prayer is
'Heaven in ordinarie...The milky way, the bird of Paradise...The land of spices'. Then, at the end, all is simplicity.
Like the still, small voice after the earthquake, wind and fire of all
these images, prayer is 'something understood'.

Up until 1629, Herbert is struggling to understand. He is lifted
up only to be thrown down. He is able to praise the church, to
enshrine its doctrine in measured syllables, yet at the same time
worry and gnaw with anxiety about his place within it. By early
1629, however, his life had changed dramatically. After the death
of his mother, a new decisiveness crept into George's life. He had
finally escaped from the responsibility of the Orator's post, and he
was free at last from financial worries. Even his health had
improved. Significantly too, he had moved to Wiltshire, where,
although he cannot have known it, he was to spend the rest of his
life. Dauntsey House, with its garden and pleasant prospects was
to be the place where he would finally come to a decision to enter

the.priesthood and where he would meet the woman who was to
be his wife.

Most of all, at some point during 1629 he came to a decision. At
some time during that year he was able to truly say to God, 'Thy
will be done.' At long last, between George Herbert and his God,
something was understood.

CHAPTER

16
1630

Baynton, Bemerton

'IN CHUSING A WIFE, AND BUYING A SWORD, WE OUGHT NOT
TO TRUST ANOTHER.'
Outlandish Proverbs No.490

Marriage

The account of George Herbert's marriage is one of the most
fantastic passages in the whole of Walton's hugely inaccurate
book. According to Walton, Charles Danvers of Baynton, a kinsman of Sir John Danvers had 'often and publickly declar'd a
desire that Mr. *Herbert* would marry any of his Nine Daughters
(for he had so many) but rather his Daughter *Jane*, than any
other, because *Jane was his beloved Daughter*'.[1] To back up his
recommendation to George, Charles Danvers praised Herbert to
his daughter so often that she 'became so much a Platonick' and
fell 'in love with Mr. *Herbert* unseen'. Thus, when Charles
Danvers died in 1626, some mutual friends introduced the couple
and three days later they were married.

This is Walton at his most hagiographic–persuading us that
Herbert's marriage was a sort of romantic minor miracle–the
lives of the saints as published by Mills and Boon. Even if we had
no documentary evidence to undermine the tale, it is probable
that George Herbert and Jane Danvers met a long time before
their marriage. For a start, Jane Danvers was Sir John's cousin; it
would have been strange if Herbert had not met her at least once
in the preceeding twenty years. Even if they had never met before
Herbert arrived in Wiltshire, Baynton House where Charles
Danvers lived was less than twenty miles from Dauntsey; it would
have been expected that he would make at least one visit to pay
his respects to his stepfather's kin. It is also extremely unlikely

that Charles Danvers, if he was so desperate about matching his daughter with 'Mr. *Herbert*', should have neglected to arrange a meeting.

The truth is, of course, much more prosaic. Documentary evidence rather destroys the story. It was customary in those days to file an 'allegation' and a 'bond' before the marriage, and these were duly filed on 23 and 26 February, the bond binding Herbert and his future brother-in-law Edward Michell (husband of Jane's sister Joan) for one hundred pounds.[2] Since the wedding took place on 5 March, if Walton is to be believed, Herbert filed these documents before he had even met the woman or known of her love for him. That Herbert was a man of faith we can believe; that he was a man of quite *that* much faith is less credible.

We can, therefore, discount Walton's version. It is far more likely that there were two deciding factors in Herbert's decision to get married. Firstly, he was now financially independent and able therefore to support a wife and family. Secondly, and somewhat obviously, his time in Wiltshire would have brought him into increased contact with the Danvers family and he probably liked what he saw.

George had previously declared in his poems his intention to remain single:

> I will not marry: or, if she be mine,
> She and her children shall be thine.
> 'The Thanksgiving'[3]

In *The Country Parson*, echoing St Paul, he was to write that, 'The Country Parson, considering that virginity is a higher state then Matrimony, and that the Ministry requires the best and highest things, is rather unmarried, then married.'[4]

Ethically, he was more inclined to remain a bachelor; so what must have swayed him, therefore, was Jane herself. Ethics, after all, become extremely flexible when you fall in love. As to the woman he married, Jane Danvers was the third daughter in a large family. Herbert certainly did not choose Jane for her money. Her father was a landowner, with property in Wiltshire and Cornwall, but with a family of fourteen, all of whom were living when he died in 1627, there cannot have been enough to make any of them a particular prize.[5]

Aubrey, with his usual mixture of bitchiness and compliment, described Jane (who was also his 'kinswoman') as 'a handsome *bona roba* and *ingeniose*'.[6] Debate has raged as to what 'bona roba' means, but he probably meant that she had an ample, well-rounded figure. Aubrey's catty comments are almost all we know of the character of Jane Danvers. Although he describes her as *ingeniose*, her skills obviously did not extend to Latin, since after the death of her husband she condemned a volume of his Latin writings 'to the uses of good housewifry', because neither she nor 'the parson of Hineham' could understand it.[7]

Her appearance must have contrasted quite startlingly with George, who according to Walton was 'inclining towards Tallness; his Body was very strait, and so far from being cumbred with too much flesh, that he was lean to an extremity.'[8] Aubrey described him likewise; 'He was a very fine complexion and consumptive,' wrote Aubrey. 'His mariage, I suppose, hastened his death.'[9]

After a brief courtship (although not quite as brief as the three days described by Walton) they were married on 5 March 1629 in the parish church of Edington, near Baynton.[10] Although Herbert had now an income, they did not have a home of their own and so the first year of their marriage was spent at Baynton House, with Jane's widowed mother and some of her brothers and sisters.

'HE THAT GIVES ME SMALL GIFTS WOULD HAVE ME LIVE.'
Outlandish Proverbs No.1000

Decision

His marriage, despite the fact that they had nowhere to live, would seem to indicate that Herbert had at last decided on his course of action. After all the years of indecision, he had decided to take the final step and become a priest.

It may be that after years of feeling forced into the priesthood, the security of his income and the death of his mother allowed him to take a more objective view. At last he was able not just to yield to God because he had no other choice, but to make a decision to let God carry him where he would. Love, when it is the only choice, is not love at all. In theory at least, he could still have rejected the priesthood. Instead–as in his poem, 'The

Pearl'–'Learning', 'Honour', and 'Pleasure' are all rejected, as Herbert is able to say 'Yet I love thee.'[11] Perhaps the alternatives now available to him served only to strengthen his decision to pay the price to secure the pearl.

Another sign that he had indeed come to an acceptance of his vocation was that on Pentecost 1629, three years after first accepting the sinecure, he preached in Lincoln Cathedral in fulfilment of his duties as prebend of Leighton Bromswold.[12] As far as we know, apart from attending his induction, this is the only time he actively fulfilled his duties. It is as if he had decided to take it all seriously, at last.

The parish which Herbert was eventually to serve became vacant some three months after his marriage, when Walter Curll became Bishop of Bath and Wells, thereby vacating a small parish with the marvellously English name of Fugglestone-cum-Bemerton. The patron of this tiny parish near Salisbury was officially the Earl of Pembroke, but because it was the King who had promoted Curll to the bishopric the gift of the living of Bemerton fell to the King.

In Walton's account, '*Philip*, then Earl of *Pembroke* requested the King to bestow it upon his kinsman *George Herbert*; and the King said, *Most willingly to Mr.* Herbert, *if it be worth his acceptance.*'[13] Herbert then, struck anew by apprehension about the job, fasted and prayed for at least a month. When his friend Arthur Woodnoth arrived to visit, Herbert had decided to turn it down. Arthur took him to Wilton House, home of the Earls of Pembroke, where the King and his entire court was assembled. Herbert told the Earl of his decision, but was persuaded otherwise by no less a personage than Bishop Laud, who saw Herbert at the behest of Philip himself.

Once again, Walton's account does not bear scrutiny. Herbert was presented with the living on 16 April 1630 and inducted ten days later. Philip did not become Earl of Pembroke until 10 April, so there was hardly enough time for a month of prayer, fasting and general indecision. Indeed, the illness and death of the third Earl would have made it impossible for the court to be anywhere near Wilton at the time. The possibility that they had all arrived to attend the funeral can be discounted, since that did not take place until 7 May, two weeks after Herbert was inducted. Whether it was Philip, the fourth Earl, or his brother and predecessor William, who petitioned the King on Herbert's behalf, it is extremely unlikely that Laud had anything to do with it, since he and Philip were sworn enemies.[14]

Once again Walton, separated from these events by the Civil War, is busy constructing an Anglican saint. In Walton's account, Herbert is not only known and esteemed by the martyr-king Charles, he has to be persuaded of his worthiness for the post by the great High Anglican Archbishop Laud.

Herbert had probably been looking for some time for a parish in Wiltshire, where he had now settled. Naturally, he would have asked William Herbert, Earl of Pembroke, as a distant relative with connections at court, to help him secure a living. George had already been in contact with William asking him for donations to the rebuilding fund for Leighton Bromswold, to which William had contributed £100.[15] When Bemerton became vacant, the living was, it is true, officially the gift of Charles, but it is hard to believe that the King would have thought twice about acceding to the wishes of William–the man who would, under any other circumstances, have given the parish away. Indeed, Charles may even have taken a wry pleasure in presenting such a tiny and unprepossessing living to the man who had once criticised his war plans.

Walton's story, therefore, is yet another fabrication. It seems clear that Herbert had decided to take the step into the priesthood at some time in 1629, certainly before he married. The time for indecision was long past.

'THE HOUSE SHEWS THE OWNER.'
Outlandish Proverbs No.8

Fugglestone-Cum-Bemerton

Herbert, as we have noted, was presented with the living on 16 April 1630, by a deed dated from Westminster.[16] On the 26th April, at Salisbury Cathedral, he was inducted into the living and the same day rode the two miles from Salisbury to Bemerton, where he was inducted into the church itself. Arthur Woodnoth and George Hulbert stood surety for him and the induction was administered by Bishop Davenant. Herbert would have known the Bishop from his Cambridge days, when Davenant was Lady Margaret Professor of Divinity and Master of Queen's College.[17]

He was still, of course, a deacon at this time. In Herbert's time, a deacon could preach, visit, catechise, baptise and marry, but he could not, of course, administer Holy Communion. It was not until 19 September that he was ordained a priest, again by Davenant.

The village of Bemerton is now almost entirely swallowed up by Salisbury. The parsonage of which Herbert took possession stood by a river, its garden sloping down towards the banks. It is a curious coincidence that one so plagued with illness as Herbert should have spent so much of his life living in damp climates. Certainly the river running along the bottom of the garden gave a pleasing prospect, but, as Walton says, the parsonage was 'more pleasant than healthful'.[18]

Both the house and the church, in fact, needed significant repairs. Herbert had to repair the chancel and rebuild almost three parts of his house which was 'fall'n down, or decayed by reason of his Predecessors living at a better Parsonage-house; namely, at *Minal*, 16 or 20 miles from this place'.[19]

There were two churches in the Parish—the tiny chapel at Bemerton and a small and undistinguished church at Fugglestone, on the edge of Wilton Park. Bemerton itself was described by Aubrey as 'a pittiful little chappell of Ease'.[20] In the light of Herbert's modern reputation, the church of St Andrews at Bemerton does indeed appear surprisingly small. Rectangular in shape, it has no tower and contains only enough seats for some thirty people. Though today it has been beautifully decorated, at the time of Herbert's acceptance of the living it must have seemed a meagre sign of the glories of becoming a man of the cloth.

According to Walton, Herbert having let himself be persuaded could hardly wait to be ordained priest. He 'long'd for the next *Ember-week*, that he might be ordain'd *priest*, and made capable of Administring both the Sacraments.'[21] If so, it was a strange kind of impatience, for he missed the first opportunity. He could have been ordained on 23 May at an ember week service at which Nathaniel Bostock, Herbert's own curate, was ordained. Instead Herbert opted to wait until the next occasion, on 19 September.[22] Why did he still hold back? It was not, we can assume, from a lack of desire. He had made his decision now and there would have been no point in trying to put off the awful moment if, indeed, that was what he believed it to be.

There are two more probable explanations. The first and most likely is that the rectory was nowhere near ready for habitation, and that Herbert did not want to take on the full responsibilities until he could live in the parish. At that time he would have been 'commuting' from Baynton, or staying at Wilton House.

Alternatively, as Amy Charles suggests, he may well have made a final journey north to Lincoln, where, along with preaching the Whitsunday service in the Cathedral as he was obliged to do, he was also hoping to persuade Nicholas Ferrar to take over the work at Leighton Bromswold. Now that he was fully committed to Bemerton, Herbert was keen that someone other than he should take responsibility for Leighton. Nicholas Ferrar himself wrote in his preface to the first edition of *The Temple* that 'As for worldly matters, his love and esteem to them was so little, as no man can more ambitiously seek, then he did earnestly endeavour the resignation of an Ecclesiasticall dignitie, which he was possessour of.'[23] In other words, he was no longer interested in sinecures, but in ensuring that someone fulfilled a living and active role as a parish priest to the people of Leighton.

John Ferrar in his biography agrees that Herbert first tried to get 'Brother Ferrar' to accept Leighton in his stead. It was Nicholas who declined this offer and suggested that George renew his attempts to rebuild the church:

> Tho' there had been gotten a Brief for the repairing of it, the Cost estimated to be at the least upon two thousand pounds, & collections yet made, the money being not above [space] pounds, could no way help the matter. N.F. very earnestly hereupon assaults his Brother Herbert, to sett to the work, & to try, what he could doe amongst his Friends, towards so good a work: N.F. promising all the assistance he could in that kind...[24]

The initial thrust to rebuild the church had obviously petered out. Herbert was to take Ferrar's advice and renew his efforts from 1631 onwards. Perhaps the expense of rebuilding his own parsonage of Bemerton meant that he still needed the income from Leighton. Either way, instead of taking on all the work of organising the rebuilding, he persuaded his brother Sir Henry

Herbert and Arthur Woodnoth to take the task on. They put together a prospectus, or list of subscribers, including their aims and intentions, which they would show to prospective donors. Henry Herbert was later to write to his brother that the Duchess of Lennox 'lik'd our book well, & has given order to yᵉ Tenants, at Leighton, to make payment of it'.[25]

Whatever the reason for his missing the earliest opportunity, for the first five months of Herbert's incumbency the parish of Bemerton had a curate who was ordained and a vicar who was not. Herbert was eventually ordained on 19 September. One of the priests who laid hands on the new ordinand was Humphrey Henchman, later Bishop of London. '*He laid his hand on Mr. Herberts Head,*' he told Walton, '*and (alas!) within less then three Years, lent his Shoulder to carry his dear Friend to his Grave.*'[26]

Those three years, if we are to believe the evidence of his contemporaries and his own quasi-autobiographical account in *The Country Parson*, were to be the happiest and most fulfilled of Herbert's life. He had his own home, a wife, and he had resolved his own conflicts.

17

1630-1632

St Andrew's, Bemerton

'IF GREAT MEN WOULD HAVE CARE OF LITTLE ONES, BOTH
WOULD LAST LONG.'
Outlandish Proverbs No.697

Adoption

In 1606 George's second sister, Margaret, had married John
Vaughan, son and heir of Owen Vaughan of Llwydiath,
Montgomeryshire. John Vaughan died in 1615–an event which
may have occasioned a rare visit by Magdalene to
Montgomeryshire. Sir Francis Newport, brother of Magdalene
and uncle to Edward, wrote to his nephew, 'Mye syster y'r
mother is confident to take a iourney into these pts this somer, the
rather I think because yo'r brother Vaugh'n is dead.'[1]

Margaret survived her husband for a further eight years until
she too died at Llanerfyl in Montgomeryshire and was buried
with the family at Montgomery Church. Three daughters survived Margaret and John: Dorothy, Magdalene and Catharine.

Now George was settled, Edward, who had been reluctantly
looking after his nieces all this time, was keen that he should take
a turn. Accordingly, as soon as George and Jane Herbert had
moved into the refurbished rectory Edward wrote to him.
George, in turn, wrote to Henry:

> I will tell you what I wrote to our eldest brother, when he
> urged one upon me, and but one, and that at my choice. I
> wrote to him that I would have both or neither; and that
> upon this ground, because they were to come into an
> unknown country, tender in knowledge, sense, and age,
> and knew none but one who could be no company to them.

> Therefore I considered that if one only came, the comfort
> intended would prove a discomfort.[2]

So Magdalene and Dorothy had come to live at the rectory,
with Herbert and his wife Jane. Herbert's wise advice proved
true, and the two girls were, indeed, company for one another:
'They have lived so lovingly, lying, eating, walking, praying,
working, still together, that I take a comfort therein.'[3]

Henry had offered to have one of the nieces himself. George
suggests the youngest sister, Catharine, for whom he appears to
have a great deal of sympathy:

> It is true there is a third sister, whom to receive were the
> greatest charitie of all, for she is youngest, and least looked
> unto; having none to doe it but her school-mistresse, and
> you know what those mercenary creatures are. Neither
> have she any to repair unto at good times, as Christmas,
> &c.... If you could think of taking her, as once you did,
> surely it were a great good deed, and I would have her
> conveyed to you.... Yet, truly if you take her not, I am
> thinking to do it, even beyond my strengthe; especially at
> this time, being more beggarly now than I have been these
> many years, as having spent two hundred pounds in
> building; which to me that have nothing yett, is very
> much.[4]

Despite the temporary poverty, occasioned by the completion
of building work on the church and rectory, Catharine joined her
sisters in the Herbert household at Bemerton. Herbert, though he
never fathered a child, now had a wife and three daughters.

The daughters formed close relationships, not only with their
uncle, but also with their aunt and her family. Baynton was only a
few miles from Bemerton and Jane must have taken the girls to
meet her family. Even though they were only at Bemerton for
three years, the relationship grew to such an extent that Dorothy
left small legacies to Jane's mother, sisters and other relatives
when she made her will in 1632.[5]

Outlandish Proverbs

When writing to Henry about their nieces, George quotes a proverb: 'But take this rule, and it is an outlandish one... "the best bredd child hath the best portion".'[6]

As has already been noted, throughout their lives, Henry and George were fascinated by proverbs and sayings. George's collection was published after his death as *Outlandish Proverbs* (1640), retitled *Jacula Prudentum* (1651).[7] Although there has been debate as to whether Herbert was really the author, or rather collector of these proverbs–to some people it seems rather a trivial interest for so great a poet–the evidence is conclusive.

In this letter, for example, George refers to one of the proverbs as 'outlandish', the very name used to entitle his first published collection. The word recurs in the collection that Henry compiled, now in the National Library of Wales, which is entitled *Outlandishe Proverbs selected out of severall Languages & enterd here the vi. August 1637 at Ribsford*. Also, among the manuscripts belonging to John Mapletoft, Nicholas Ferrar's godson, was 'a large book of stories, with outlandish proverbs at the end, englished by Mr Geo Herbert: in all, 463 proverbs'.[8] Herbert as an orator and preacher realised the value of carefully chosen, pithy sayings and aphorisms. 'Sometimes he tells them stories, and sayings of others,' he wrote of the good preacher in *The Country Parson*, 'for them also men heed, and remember better then exhortations.'[9] He even used such devices in his verse. Poems such as 'Charmes and Knots' are really just collections of proverbs.

Perhaps the brothers' love of proverbs began, as Amy Charles suggests, when they were learning languages using collections of French sayings. Or perhaps it began for Herbert at Westminster School, where among the mass of religious observance, every day began with a lesson from the book of Proverbs. Either way, this interest in 'outlandish', and often just plain ridiculous, proverbs reflects Herbert's love of brevity. His early poems, such as 'The Church Militant' and 'The Church Porch', and especially Latin works such as *Lucus* or *Passio Discerpta* are tortuously long. By 1627, however, he was extolling the virtues of succinctness to his successor as Orator, recommending that orations should be 'brief and concise'.[10] As he matured as a poet, he not only turned to the shorter lyric and sonnet forms for which he is best remembered, but also sought out emblems, symbols and word patterns to express a mass of meaning in a simple image.

There was always something of the don about Herbert. His passion for proverbs is a typically scholarly pastime, and his delight in word-games also reflects something of the scholar. His poetry is littered with puns and puzzles, anagrams and acrostics.

Such devices are most noticeable, of course, in his 'picture poems'. Poems like 'The Altar' where the words on the page form the shape of an altar, are typical of a kind of donnish, almost mathematical love of clever word-play. 'Easter-wings', is another poem, where the two verses form the shapes of two wings. More poems are shaped almost mathematically: 'Trinitie Sunday' for example is a visual pun on the Trinity, three verses of three lines each. The last stanza even has three subjects to each line:

> Enrich my heart, mouth, hands in me,
>   With faith, with hope, with charitie;
>   That I may runne, rise, rest with thee.[11]

Examples abound. The 'Anagram of the Virgin Mary' plays entirely on the army/Mary anagram. 'Coloss. 3.3.' is an acrostic, where the verse, 'My life is hid in him that is my treasure' runs diagonally down the poem. 'Jesu' is punned as 'I ease you', 'Love-Joy' puns the initials of Jesus Christ with the words 'Joy' and 'Charity'. 'Sinnes Round' is a chain verse, where the last line of each verse is the first line of the next, and the last line of the poem is also the first line of the poem. 'A Wreath' takes a similar form, but with each line beginning with the last word of the previous line. These may have been inspired by Donne's 'Corona' sequence of sonnets. Herbert would surely have seen the sequence when Donne sent it to Magdalene in 1608.

'Paradise' is a word-game where the addition, or subtraction of a letter makes another word:

> I blesse thee, Lord, because I GROW
> Among thy trees, which in a ROW
> To thee both fruit and order OW.[12]

'Heaven' uses the Jacobean cliché of the 'echo' poem where the
final syllable or syllables of each line are 'echoed' back to give a
reply. This device was used throughout Jacobean literature–
Edward's poem, 'Echo in a Church' is very similar in tone.[13]
There is even an entire scene in Webster's *The Duchess of Malfi*
based around the conceit. 'The Clasping of Hands' is one long,
tedious series of puns and inversions of the words 'mine' and
'thine'. 'The Water-Course' contains alternative endings to each
line.

Perhaps Herbert's attitude to his language is best summed up
in his poem, 'The Sonne':

> I like our language, as our men and coast:
> Who cannot dresse it well, want wit, not words.
> How neatly doe we give one onely name
> To parents issue and the sunnes bright starre![14]

The remainder of the poem is a rather laboured pun on sun/
son/son of man.

'I like our language.' There was always this element in Herbert's versing. Amidst the visions of glory and the cries of pain,
there is also a fanciful word-play, a delight with words themselves, what they sound like, what one can turn them into, even
what shape they make on the page. He had a childish amusement
in puns and clever typography. In Victorian times he would have
been another Lewis Carroll, writing poems that dwindle like the
tail of a mouse. In more recent times, one can imagine him as one
of those donnish practitioners of the detective story, or a compiler
of *The Times* crossword.

Such devices and tricks did not always receive universal
acclaim. Professor Tuve demonstrates that much of Herbert's
'originality' was in fact, commonplace to his contemporaries.
Certainly in later years, particularly in the eighteenth century,
Herbert was dismissed as a trivial writer, who 'liked to perform
stunts and toy with oddities'.[15] Such attitudes are best summed
up in Dryden's attack in 'MacFlecknoe':

> Thy genius calls thee not to purchase fame
> In keen Iambicks, but mild Anagram:
> Leave writing Plays, and chuse for thy command
> Some peaceful Province in Acrostic Land.

> There thou maist wings display and Altars raise,
> And torture one poor word Ten thousand ways.[16]

He underestimates the skill with which Herbert applies these techniques, for later authors who tried their hands at such tricks were not nearly so successful. Usually their poems are overwhelmed by their own cleverness. Like one of those films where millions have been spent on the special effects, with no thought for the storyline or characterisation, the content does not live up to the packaging.

There are, of course, times when the same fate befalls Herbert, when the 'cleverness' overwhelms the poem entirely, but such moments are comparatively rare. One of the strengths of Herbert as a poet is that his poems not only survive this kind of treatment, but are even enriched by them. 'The Altar', for example, achieves greatness, not *despite* the trick played with the typography, nor *because* of it, but because the craftsman in Herbert achieves the delicate balance between poetic content and the eye-catching 'special effect'. Herbert was not trying to shock. He was not being clever for the sake of cleverness. The shape of his poems, the physical structure, is part and parcel of the poem itself. At its best, it imbues the poem with an almost sculptural physicality. Even when the attempt is not quite so successful, there is often a kind of *joie de vivre* about it – a sense of playfulness and joy in the possibilities that words offer us.

'WHERE THERE IS PEACE, GOD IS.'
Outlandish Proverbs No.733

Life at Bemerton

Now aged 37, Herbert had a wife and family. Together they lived in the rectory, with its orchard leading down to the River Nadder and at the bottom of the garden they could look across the water meadows to Salisbury Cathedral. It was only a short walk along the river bank to the cathedral close, a walk that Herbert took many times. He was now settled into the familiar round of services, visiting, pastoral care, christenings, weddings and funerals that has been the job of every parson before and since.

The people for whom he had responsibility ranged from the

lowest vagrant to the noble residents of nearby Wilton House. Most of them, however, were the typical village labourers of the time: hard-working, often stubbornly superstitious and generally illiterate. It was the superstition that most worried the ecclesiastical authorities.

In 1626, for example, the appointment of a zealous Protestant vicar in the parish of Eccleston in Lancashire led to prosecutions for bowling in service time, superstitious burning of candles, blessing sick cattle and using invocations on the bodies of men and beasts.[17] He even secured prosecution for a parishioner who had dipped the child into the font after it had been baptised at the minister's hands, a throwback to the Catholic tradition of immersing the baby. This practice had been replaced by the sprinkling of water on the baby's head. The fact that the clergy now had families of their own brought home to them the discomfort and distress caused by plunging the baby in the ice cold water of the font.[18]

Such 'superstition' proved extremely difficult to remove, backed up as it was by the literal-mindedness of ignorance:

> In 1631, Mr Sherfield... having long observed 'many people' pause and bow before a window in his parish church at Salisbury, asked them why they did so. 'Because the Lord our God is there,' was the reply. On looking more closely into the glass, 'all diamonded with quaint device,' he found that it contained seven representations of God the Father in the form of a little old man with a blue and red coat, with a pouch at his side.[19]

The church courts were re-established to prosecute such superstitious errors, along with the more mundane moral lapses, such as drunkenness, and sexual immorality for which offenders were forced to do penance in front of their neighbours and kinfolk.[20]

In practice, the efficiency of such courts depended almost entirely on the standing of the minister. At Keevil in Wiltshire, the minister's attempt to suppress the summer revels of 1611 only resulted in his parishioners singing an obscene libel at him. In the end, he seems to have settled for a more reasonable standard of church observance.[21] Law-enforcement was clearly not the answer. One of the hard lessons learned in the years of the

Commonwealth was that you could not legislate for godliness. Banning wrong would not automatically result in right.

Instead, the answer lay in the example set by the clergy themselves. As a parson, Herbert was in many ways typical of a new breed. In the decades preceding Herbert's ordination, the clergy had never been noted for their piety or even intellectual ability. Part of this was due to the low income that went with the job. In 1585, Archbishop Whitgift reported that out of 9,000 benefices, over half had incomes of less than £10 per annum. Since the Reformation, the clergy could marry and raising families on such incomes caused much hardship. Parsons were undertrained and underfunded and put in charge of a flock, most of whom could neither read nor write. Small wonder then that standards were difficult to maintain.

The want of money encouraged clergy to pluralism – the taking on of more than one parish – and pluralism meant that in one or other of the parishes, the vicar was non-resident. Even where there was a resident clergyman, their behaviour, especially the behaviour of those in the Salisbury diocese, was sometimes less decorous than might be expected. One such parson returned drunk from Salisbury, and instead of hearing the catechisms of all the girls waiting for him in the church gave them all a kiss and a 'tuttye' or nosegay.[22]

In the years preceding Herbert's ordination, therefore, strenuous efforts had been made to attract new blood into the ministry. Standards improved, both in the numbers of clergy and in their educational qualifications. In Worcester, for example, 52% of the clergy were graduates by 1620, compared to only 23% in 1580.[23]

Part of the reason for this need was the Protestant emphasis on preaching. The new doctrines had to be taken to the people and, since the mass of the population were illiterate, they would have to be told. Efforts were therefore undertaken not only to improve the quality of the clergy, but also to establish a powerful preaching ministry. Of course, it didn't always work. Some parsons rather overdid the teaching, like the Wiltshire parson whose sermons were described by one girl as, 'such a deale of bibble babble that I am weary to hear yt and I can then sitt downe in my seat and take a good napp'.[24]

By 1630 a resident, educated clergy had emerged for the first time. The product of the universities, they brought to many villages skills in oratory and logic, along with the benefit of their libraries and their intellectual ability.[25] They still, however, had much to learn about dealing with a people often vastly different from themselves. Such was the background to Herbert's manual for country clergy, *The Country Parson*.

'A HANDFUL OF GOOD LIFE IS BETTER THEN A BUSHELL OF
LEARNING.'
Outlandish Proverbs No.3

The Country Parson

The Country Parson, as many critics are keen to remind us, is not an autobiography. It is instead a manual, an ideal, or, as Herbert himself called it, 'a Mark to aim at'. Even so, it is foolish to go to the other extreme and think that there is no autobiography in it, that it is some kind of clerical Utopia. No man could write a book like this unless he were living to some extent the life he describes within. To do otherwise would be simply to hold oneself up to ridicule. 'By their fruits ye shall know them,' Herbert would have read in his Bible.[26] There must, therefore, be a great deal in the book which is taken straight from the fruits of Herbert's life at Bemerton.

Certainly Barnabas Oley, the book's first editor, believed that Herbert had largely lived the life he described. '*His* practice it was, and *His Character* it is, *His* as *Authour*, and *His* as *Object*'.[27] Oley also gave the book its 'official' title of *A Priest to the Temple*. The book was not published until 1670, and Oley was aiming to tie it in with the previously published collection of poems, *The Temple*. Most readers today, however, know it simply by the more prosaic, and certainly more fitting, title, *The Country Parson*.

> I have resolved to set down the Form and Character of a
> true Pastour, that I may have a Mark to aim at: which also
> I will set as high as I can, since hee shoots higher that
> threatens the Moon, then hee that aims at a Tree.[28]

So begins the book, (including a typical Herbert proverb) but despite his description of it as a 'target', it was clearly not written until some time into Herbert's ministry as a 'pastour'. The book was completed in 1632, two years after Herbert had taken up residency at Bemerton and contains characters and scenes which he could only have discovered once he had begun his role.

Chapter II–'The Parson's Life'–sets the tone for the book:

> The Countrey Parson is exceeding exact in his Life, being holy, just, prudent, temperate, bold, grave in all his wayes...he labours most in those things which are most apt to scandalize his Parish. And first, because Countrey people live hardly, and therefore as feeling their own sweat, and consequently knowing the price of mony, are offended much with any, who by hard usage increase their travell...'[29]

The Parson should, then, avoid luxury ('a very visible sin') and drunkenness and make sure that his word is his bond: 'Countrey people...do much esteem their word...therefore the Parson is very strict in keeping his word...The Parsons yea is yea, and nay nay.'[30]

Indeed, simplicity and discipline are the keynotes of the book. The lifestyle of the parson should be simple. His furniture is 'very plain, but clean, whole, and sweet, as sweet as his garden can make, for he hath no mony for such things'. His food is 'plain and common, but wholesome, what hee hath, is little, but very good.'[31] He should be dressed simply but cleanly, 'his apparell plaine, but reverend, and clean, without spots, or dust, or smell; the purity of his mind breaking out, and dilating it selfe even to his body, cloaths, and habitation'.[32]

Amidst the instructions and advice, Herbert paints wonderful pictures of his congregation:

> Besides his example, he having often instructed his people how to carry themselves in divine service, exacts of them all possible reverence, by no means enduring either talking, or sleeping, or gazing, or leaning, or halfe-kneeling, or any undutifull behaviour in them...and every one, man, and child, answering aloud both Amen, and all other answers...which answers also are to be done not in a hudling, or slubbering fashion, gaping or scratching the

head, or spitting even in the midst of their answer, but
gently and pausably...[33]

He pays much attention to the need for a Parson to have
read not only the Scriptures, but 'Commenters and
Fathers...Wherefore he hath one Comment at least upon every
book of Scripture...'[34] The reason for this is exactly the need
outlined above: to equip the Parson for teaching and preaching.
'The Countrey Parson preacheth constantly, the pulpit is his joy
and his throne.'[35]

The chapter entitled, 'The Parson Preaching' is fascinating,
not only for the insight it gives us into Herbert's own preaching
technique but also for the general rules which are as relevant
today as they were four hundred years ago. The parson is to be
specific, for 'particulars touch, and awake more than generalls'.
He is also to be inventive and imaginative:

> Sometimes he tells them stories, and sayings of
> others...for them also men heed, and remember better
> then exhortations; which though earnest, yet often dy with
> the Sermon, especially with Countrey people; which are
> thick and heavy, and hard to raise to a poynt of Zeal...

The style of preaching of Herbert's day was heavily influenced
by the rhetoric and logic taught in the universities – teaching that
he himself had been a part of. Pedantic, learned, and utterly
remote from the kind of people Herbert was preaching to every
week, he now condemned this style:

> Whereas the other way of crumbling a text into small parts,
> as, the Person speaking, or spoken to, the subject, and
> object, and the like, hath neither in it sweetnesse, nor
> gravity, nor variety, since the words apart are not
> Scripture, but a dictionary.[36]

Above all, sermons were to be challenging: 'He often tels
them, that Sermons are dangerous things, that none goes out of
Church as he came in, but either better or worse...he is not
witty, or learned, or eloquent, but Holy.'[37]
Nothing could be more indicative of the distance Herbert had
journeyed from his days as University Orator, when wit and

eloquence were all and when holiness was definitely not required. He ends with possibly the most practical point of all: 'The Parson exceeds not an hour in preaching.'

The Country Parson is a treasure trove of advice and illustration. With its homely style, its simple, direct instruction, and sprinkled with his beloved 'outlandish' proverbs, it provides a unique insight into Herbert's life at Bemerton. His experience of repairing the church is brought into chapter XIII, 'The Parson's Church':

> Therefore first he takes order, that all things be in good repair; as walls plaistered, windows glazed, floore paved, seats whole, firm and uniform, especially that the Pulpit, and Desk, and Communion Table, and Font be as they ought, for those great duties that are performed in them.[38]

The Country Parson, however, contains far more than is merely applicable to the clergy. It seems clear that Herbert was recording his way of life. Chapters on marriage, good husbandry, the management of servants, parental discipline and medicine mingle with chapters on preaching, visiting, catechising and administering the sacraments.

Perhaps the 'broadest' of all the chapters is 'The Parson's Survey', where Herbert's view ranges beyond the borders of the tiny village and into the nation as a whole:

> The Countrey Parson hath not onely taken a particular Survey of the faults of his own Parish, but a generall also of the diseases of the time...[39]

It clearly draws on Herbert's own experiences, with its advice to 'Heirs or younger Brothers':

> Sometimes he may go to Court, as the eminent place both of good and ill...When there is a Parliament he is to endeavour by all means to be a Knight or Burgess there; for there is no school to a Parliament. And when he is there, he must not only be a morning man, but at Committees also; for there the particulars are exactly discussed, which are brought from thence to the House but in generall.[40]

The wheel has turned full circle. Herbert was now in a position to look back on his life and pick out the good and bad. Nowhere are preferment, glory or honour mentioned. Instead such experiences are training for the real task in life, the task of inducing in man 'the Obedience of God'. It is a task with both duty and dignity.

> The Dignity, in that a Priest may do that which Christ did, and by his auctority, and as his Viceregent. The Duty, in that a Priest is to do that which Christ did, and after his manner, both for Doctrine and Life.[41]

The dignity of the job was very important to Herbert, for he was living in an age when the priesthood was still looked down upon. He had, as had Ferrar, been mocked for losing himself 'in an humble way'.[42] It is a charge he has grown to expect:

> The Countrey Parson knows well, that both for the generall ignominy which is cast upon the profession, and much more for those rules, which out of his choysest judgment hee hath resolved to observe, and which are described in this Book, he must be despised; because this hath been the portion of God his Master . . . and this is foretold, it shall be so still until things be no more.[43]

The only way to counter such contempt is through a 'holy and unblameable life' and that is what the book is really all about. To view it purely as a manual for seventeenth-century clerics is to miss the heart of the book. *The Country Parson* is not, primarily, about being a priest; it is about being holy. Its call is therefore to all people in general, as well as priests in particular, to live their lives as an example to others, to *be* rather than merely to talk about, the Word of God.

18

Bemerton

'THE ITCH OF DISPUTING IS THE SCAB OF THE CHURCH.'
Jacula Prudentum No.1137

George Herbert–High or Low Church?

What *The Country Parson* does not tell us is the precise nature of
Herbert's theological position. Even if he had made it clear, it is
difficult to imagine that it would have stemmed the tide of spec-
ulation that has raged ever since. Heroes–especially religious
heroes–have a habit of being claimed by followers of vastly
differing persuasions.

The fact is that ever since his death, all sides have claimed, and
still claim, that Herbert was one of their own. 'The religious wars
of the seventeenth century,' writes one observer 'are being re-
fought by twentieth-century literary critics.'[1]

The problem is that so much of our perception of Herbert's
position within the church of his time comes from the attitudes of
his early biographers. The editor of *The Country Parson*, Barnabas
Oley, had been a student at Cambridge where he no doubt
attended Herbert's lectures and listened to his orations. Along
with being the vicar of Great Gransden, Huntingdonshire, Oley
was a fellow of Clare College, but his High Church sympathies
brought him into increasing trouble in the years of the Civil War.
He was ejected from his fellowship in 1644 by the Earl of Manchester, the Puritan who had been sent to reform the university.

Oley spent the Civil War as part of the Royalist political
underground. After wandering penniless for seven years, he settled down in the north of England and took on the task of editing
George Herbert's *Remains*.[2] The first edition of this work–which
also contained *Jacula Prudentum*, some letters of Herbert and his

Latin poems to Donne and Bacon—was published in 1652, with an anonymous preface.[3] Oley could not reveal he was the editor, because his position as a 'wanted man' would have rendered the book unpublishable. From his perspective as a fugitive in the heart of the Commonwealth, Herbert appeared to Oley as a golden-age ideal, a High Anglican priest whose call was not only to holy living, but to a specific ecclesiastical viewpoint.

Such an attitude is echoed in Herbert's successors. Later poets, such as Henry Vaughan, saw Herbert as a figure of 'pre-revolutionary piety' who was obviously and unquestionably on the side of William Laud and King Charles I.[4] With his hagiography, Walton merely provided the *coup de grace*. After his *Life*, it took three centuries before the traditional High Church view of Herbert was seriously challenged. Herbert is almost guilty by association. He *must* be High Church, because those who write about him are of that persuasion.

The truth is not so simple. If High Church poets admired Herbert, then Puritans like Edward Taylor were equally inspired.[5] It is interesting to note that every one of Herbert's supporters were anti-Laudians and therefore unsympathetic, to varying degrees, to High Churchmanship. Bishop Williams was an avowed enemy of Laud, as was Philip Herbert, Duke of Pembroke. Indeed, on 12 April 1630, only a few weeks before Herbert obtained the living of Bemerton, Laud had beaten Philip Herbert in a bitterly contested election for the post of Chancellor of Oxford. Even Herbert's bishop, John Davenant, was an anti-Laudian, having incurred the great man's wrath for a sermon on predestination, as well as for supporting schemes for Protestant union.[6]

Laud was no crypto-Catholic, but when he became Archbishop of Canterbury the reforms he set in place were certainly intended to reinforce the liturgical and symbolic, at the expense of exposition and preaching. A 'little low, red faced man of mean parentage', his contemporaries nicknamed him 'Little Laud'. He was a political street-fighter, who had fought his way up from humble beginnings to a position of power and prestige. What Laud wanted more than anything else was unity; and unity meant having the altar in the right place, wearing the right vestments and everyone chanting the same lines.[7] Preaching came under special attack. Puritan lecturers were banned, and ordained ministers were instructed not to preach on controversial subjects.[8]

Herbert was undeniably committed to the Anglican Church, but he was not necessarily as 'high' as many would have us believe. *The Country Parson* is strong in its approval of using the sign of the cross in infant baptism–an action which was dismissed as ceremonial mumbo-jumbo by the Puritans; but it is equally strong in its emphasis on preaching, the explosive effects of which Arminians at that time were trying to diffuse. He expounds a strongly sabbatarian doctrine–again a shibboleth of the Puritans– yet he also defends the country customs. Laud insisted on ritual and liturgy as an end in itself. It was enough that men performed the same thing at the same time. Herbert never mistook the means for the end. The symbols were always just that; *symbols*, signs to point people to deeper truths.

In *Musae Responsoriae*, Herbert's only direct dispute with the Puritans, he defended the rituals and symbols attacked by Melville, but forebore to attack Calvin or Calvinist theology.[9] Herbert was in fact a Calvinist, a believer in predestination, but then so were many people in the Anglican Church at this time. It was only centuries later that the name of Calvin became associated with a sort of rigid nonconformity. The theme can be found in 'The Church-Militant', with its vision of a predestined history of the Church, right through to Judgement Day; as well as in 'The Water-Course':

$$\text{Who [God] gives to man, as he sees fit,} \begin{cases} \text{Salvation} \\ \text{Damnation}^{10} \end{cases}$$

The Arminianism of Laud and Charles, which maintained, in Burton's words, 'that we have free-will of our selves', was clearly not a position which Herbert could easily hold.[11]

The truth is that the lines of distinction between 'high' and 'low' did not become rigidly formalised until after Laud's accession to the See of Canterbury in 1633. Even then there was a considerable amount of fluidity.[12] Herbert certainly believed and supported the ritual and rite of the Book of Common Prayer, but his reputation as the poet of the Anglican Church tends to over-emphasise his view of liturgy and forget that he had a typically 'low-church' view of the Bible. The Scriptures were that in which all of his faith, and, indeed his poetry, was steeped. The Bible was the 'Word', which 'hath the precedence even of Revelations and Visions'.[13] As a poet he loved and revered symbols, as an academic he also trusted written evidence. Even his published work fell foul of the Anglican censors on more than one occasion. When Ferrar tried to publish *The Temple*, it was held up by the censors because of the lines in 'The Church Militant':

> Religion stands on tip-toe in our Land
> Readie to pass to the *American* strand[14]

Only two years after this, the Puritan preacher Samuel Ward was imprisoned for uttering remarks almost identical to the lines which caused such trouble.[15]

And so in as much as we can determine anything of his theology, all we discover is that Herbert was typical of the churchmen of his day. It is tempting to think of churches of those days as full of either happy, laughing, High Anglican Cavaliers or dour, black-suited Puritans, but the picture is simply wrong.[16]

Most people, like Herbert, pursued the *via media*. The middle road, however, was not a narrow path but a broad motorway, with almost as many lanes as there were travellers.[17] Such lanes were frequently crossed and recrossed and a man might be considered both Arminian and Puritan. Those who 'retired', who kept their opinions to themselves, were always suspect. Traditional wisdom, for example, links Ferrar and Herbert together as two Anglo Catholic divines, but in his own day, Ferrar inspired admiration and distrust from both sides. Little Gidding was an 'Arminian nunnery' to those who took a dim view of the night watches and fasts and of the decorated chapels, organ music and candles. Yet Laudians also distrusted Ferrar. He was a friend of Williams, he had the communion table in the 'low' position, he described the Pope as 'the Antichrist'. One visitor described Ferrar and his family as, 'orthodox, regular, puritan protestants'.[18] Ferrar himself hated such assertions and accusations. He was 'torn asunder as with mad horses, or crushed betwixt the upper and under milstone of contrary reports, that he was a Papist, and that he was a Puritan'.[19]

Like many of his countrymen, Herbert chose to ignore the 'curious questions and divisions' which so exercised the mind of his contemporaries. He did not live to see the introduction of many of Laud's reforms and regimentations, so it is impossible to guess which side of the fence he would have been on. All we can do is agree with Ilona Bell when she says that, 'It is obvious that George Herbert believed in the Church of England, but it is far less obvious what he thought members of the Church of England should believe.'[20]

Whatever his beliefs, he would surely have detested the hardening of those doctrinal lines into political dogma. The Civil War split apart not only his own family, but also his circle of friends. Among those who laboured to rebuild Leighton Bromswold, for example, John Ferrar joined the Royalist cause and Arthur Woodnoth the Parliamentarian. Old friends were forced to choose not only different lanes, but different roads entirely.

19

Bemerton, Salisbury, Wilton

'IN THE HOUSE OF A FIDLER, ALL FIDDLE.'
Outlandish Proverbs No.223

Music

One benefit Herbert's life at Bemerton gave him in abundance
was the chance to listen to, and take part in, church music.

He lived in an age where liturgical music was flourishing. For
Herbert, it was a source of encouragement and enlightenment, a
way out of the pits of depression, a stairway to God. 'If I travell in
your companie,' he wrote in his poem 'Church-Musick', 'You
know the way to heavens doore.'[1]

All his life he had a passion for music. The *Kitchen Booke* kept
by Magdalene Herbert during the first years of their stay in
Charing Cross demonstrates as we have seen, that the family
knew famous composers like Bull and Byrd.[2] At Westminster,
Salisbury and Cambridge Herbert would have heard their elaborate polyphonic settings of the liturgy. Just as important to him
though, was the music used for private devotion, simple arrangements of voices and instruments. He learned an instrument at a
very early age, as did all his family. His brother Edward was an
accomplished lutenist, whose 'Lute-book' in the Fitzwilliam
Museum contains not only his own compositions but settings by
composers such as John Dowland.[3] Dowland and his followers
made popular the 'air' in England, the secular music which
enabled the setting of much longer lyrics. It has been estimated
that a quarter of the poems in *The Temple* are directly concerned
in some way with music:[4]

Consort both heart and lute, and twist a song

159

> Pleasant and long:
> Or, since all musick is but three parts vied
> And multiplied,
> O let they blessed Spirit bear a part,
> And make up our defects with his sweet art.[5]

At Bemerton Herbert had the chance to indulge his passion to the full. Walton tells us that his 'chiefest recreation was Musick, in which heavenly Art he was a most excellent Master, and did himself compose many *divine Hymns* and *Anthems*, which he set and sung to his *Lute* or *Viol*...'[6] Aubrey too, recalls that 'H. Allen, of Dantsey, was well acquainted with him, who has told me that he had a very good hand on the Lute, and that he sett his own Lyricks or sacred poems.'[7]

Music, then, was part of his life. It formed an integral part of his own church services. Some vicars, along with the metrical psalms, introduced hymn books such as Miles Coverdale's *Goastly Psalmes and Spiritual Songs* or George Wither's *Hymns and Songs of the Church*.[8] With Salisbury so close, Herbert took every opportunity to go and listen to the music in the great cathedral and take part in music meetings:

> Yet his love to *Musick* was such, that he went usually twice every week on certain appointed days, to the *Cathedral Church* in *Salisbury*...But before his return thence to *Bemerton*, he would usually sing and play his part, at an appointed private Musick-meeting...[9]

As Herbert sat there, listening to the 'singing men of Sarum' at the cathedral, their plainsong and choral services accompanied by the organ and augmented by boy choristers, he cannot have known that these same singing men would sing at his own funeral.

'LIFE WITHOUT A FRIEND IS DEATH WITHOUT A WITNESSE.'
Outlandish Proverbs No.385

Arthur Woodnoth

One of the most frequent visitors at Bemerton was Arthur Wood-noth, who was a cousin of Nicholas Ferrar and, as we have seen,

Sir John Danver's business manager. Walton describes Arthur Woodnoth as follows:

> He was a man, that had consider'd, overgrown Estates do often require more care and watchfulness to preserve, than get them, and consider'd that there be many Discontents, that Riches cure not; and did therefore set limits to himself as to desire of wealth: And having attain'd so much as to be able to shew some mercy to the Poor, and preserve a competence for himself, he dedicated the remaining part of his life to the service of God; and to be useful to his friends: and he proved to be so to Mr. *Herbert*.[10]

Woodnoth, in other words, was a self-made business man, whose wealth allowed him to devote his time to helping others. He was a goldsmith and banker of Foster Lane in London, who acted as a purchasing agent for the community at Little Gidding, buying them whatever supplies they needed from the Capital. He had also been a member of the Virginia Company, which was probably where he had come into contact with Sir John.[11] Perhaps it was on Arthur's advice that Sir John later sent his godson to be taught at the school at Little Gidding.[12]

Arthur Woodnoth was the same age as Herbert and it was probably he who was Walton's main source for his life of Herbert. However, there was a long gap between their conversations and the writing of the *Life*, for Woodnoth died in 1644 and the *Life* was not written until 1670. In the first edition, Walton, with the scrupulous scholarship for which he is renowned, even got Woodnoth's first name wrong.

A little while after becoming Sir John's business manager, perhaps inspired by the example of Herbert and Ferrar, Woodnoth began to examine his own life. Was he too, called to the priesthood? He appears to have asked both Ferrar and Herbert for their opinions and both advised him to continue with his present course. In a document entitled 'Reasons for Arthur Woodnoth's living with Sir John Danvers', Herbert passed his advice:

> It is a different thing to advize you now, & before you took Sr Johns affairs. you haue bin at charges: you haue stockd the grounds: you haue layed out thoughts & prayers[:] you have sowed. therfore Expect a harvest.[13]

The harvest, however, was not to be found in his work for Sir John Danvers which was frustrating and unsuccessful. 'When two things dislike you: the one for the nature thereof (as your trade) the other only for the success (as assistance of Sr John) doe as David did: putt your self into ye hands of God,' advised Herbert.

It certainly cannot have been easy being the business manager of a man so addicted to spending as Sir John Danvers, but if Ferrar is right, Arthur was prone to be too easily discouraged. It is possible that Woodnoth's 'calling' was merely the result of an unsuccessful time as Sir John's business manager.[14]

Another reason for his consideration of the priesthood seems to have been the idea that a trade was not a holy enough profession. This was not Herbert's view. 'For any scruple of leaving y^r trade, throw it away,' he wrote. 'When we exort people to continue in their vocation, it is in opposition to idlenesse. work rather than doe nothing... but a Trade having two things, the one imployment, the other profitt, the work I may change, the profitt I am master of.'

Woodnoth sent this document to Ferrar for his comments (it appears to have been Ferrar's idea that he talk to Herbert in the first place). He also reported that Herbert had said that 'we were much troubled about words for the Name of a Diuine wold satisfy all when in truth I might doo the office tho I wanted the tytle for to be a prompter of good to Sr Iohn was to be a good Angell too him Nay was to doo that which God himselfe did.'[15] To Herbert, all men could be something of a priest, just as all men were called to be holy.

'THE RICH KNOWES NOT WHO IS HIS FRIEND.'
Outlandish Proverbs No.865

Lady Anne Clifford

The Parish of Fuggleston-cum-Bemerton ran up to the gates of Wilton House itself, home of Philip, Earl of Pembroke. In *The Country Parson*, Herbert wrote about the relationship between the parson and members of the aristocracy:

> After a man is once Minister, he cannot agree to come into any house, where he shall not exercise what he is, unlesse

he forsake his plough, and look back. Wherfore they are not to be over-submissive, and base, but to keep up with the Lord and Lady of the house, and to preserve a boldness with them and all, even so farre as to reproofe to their very face, when occasion cals, but seasonably and discreetly. They who do not thus, while they remember their earthly Lord, do much forget their heavenly; they wrong the Priesthood, neglect their duty, and shall be so farre from that which they seek with their over-submissivenesse, and cringings, that they shall ever be despised. They who for the hope of promotion neglect any necesarry admonition, or reproofe, sell (with *Judas*) their Lord and Master.[16]

It is one of the strongest passages in the book. The message is clear–Herbert had played his part in such 'cringings'. He was now serving a higher court.

Woodnoth records that, at the same time he journeyed to Bemerton to discuss his own future, he went with Herbert to Wilton, where he spent a solitary hour, while Herbert spoke with the Countess of Pembroke.[17]

This is probably the basis of the rumour that Aubrey recorded, that Herbert was 'Chapelaine to Philip, Earl of Pembroke and Montgomery, and Lord Chamberlayn'.[18] There is no documentary evidence that such an arrangement was ever made official. Nevertheless, Herbert undoubtedly served as a counsellor and spiritual adviser to Lady Anne Clifford, as this reference by Woodnoth and a surviving letter show.

Perhaps Lady Anne reminded Herbert of his mother. She was cultured and learned and, like Magdalene, friendly with John Donne. We know very little of the friendship between Herbert and Lady Anne. At any rate, it cannot have been a long friendship, for Herbert was only at Bemerton for three years, and during much of that time Lady Anne was at Court. What we do know is that she was deeply unhappy. She had married Philip on 1 June 1630. She was 40 years old, and the widow of Richard Sackville, third Earl of Dorset. A remarkably able and intelligent woman, she wrote an autobiography which details, among other things, how, in the midst of a cold and sterile marriage, she made 'good Bookes and vertuous thoughts my Companions'. She needed them. Philip was 'coarse and violent and faithless'; in the end she left him in 1635.[19] 'The marble pillars of Knole in Kent and Wilton in Wiltshire were to me oftentimes but the gay arbours of anguish' she wrote.[20]

A letter to her from Herbert thanks her for a gift of a bottle of 'Metheglin'–a local brew of spiced mead, made with herbs and honey. Herbert returns his thanks, along with 'a Priests blessing, though it be none of the Court-stile, yet doubtless Madam can do you no hurt'. He is jesting. No-one knew better than the ex-Orator what the 'Court-stile' was and how to use it.[21]

In 1643 she succeeded to the vast wealth and estates of the last Earl of Cumberland and the rest of her life was devoted to the management of her estates and her many building projects. One story from her later life illustrates her strength, determination, and generous good humour. A certain tenant's rent included the yearly payment of a hen, which he generally failed to hand over. Lady Anne brought the full majesty of the law to bear on this renegade, paying over £400 to prosecute and win her case. She received the hen, cooked it and invited the tenant to dinner.[22]

Lady Anne died in 1676 at the ripe old age of 87. She did, however, pay one lasting tribute to her erstwhile spiritual adviser. In the 'great painting' which she commissioned for Appleby Castle in 1646, her love of books is demonstrated by the many volumes crowding the shelves, including works by Donne, Sidney and the vicar who had advised her during the dark days of her life: George Herbert.[23]

His time at Bemerton, therefore, in no way drew Herbert into a backwater. It was, if anything, more real than the painted world of the court and the power-politics of Parliament. In a strange way, the obscurity of Bemerton had put him in touch again with the world of the court, the world of the Lord Chamberlain. Though the 'sober men' claimed he had failed to make good use of his talents, he was using them to the full.[24] His severe criticism of chaplains who 'sell...their Lord and Master' shows how far he had come from caring about court life and preferment. Always a proud man, he had found a new kind of pride–the pride to be found in serving God.

20

Bemerton, Little Gidding

'AUTUMNALL AGUES ARE LONG, OR MORTALL.'
Outlandish Proverbs No.148

Final Illness

One Friday, early in 1633, Joshua Mapletoft arrived at Little Gidding. Mapletoft was the Vicar of Margaretting in Essex and husband of Susannah, Nicholas Ferrar's niece. He brought with him news from Bemerton.

Joshua had probably been to Bemerton to deliver a book; the first Little Gidding story book, a recollection of discussions and debates which the Little Academy had held in the winter of 1630/31. The book had been sent from Gidding to his wife and she had sent it on to Herbert.[1] When he arrived at Bemerton, and made his way to the bedroom overlooking the River Nadder, however, Joshua found Herbert gravely ill.

That he had been ill for some time was not news to the community at Little Gidding, for special prayers for his health had been said throughout the previous winter.[2] Indeed, Herbert had been so incapacitated that, by October 1632, he had to take on an additional curate because he was unable to fulfil his duties. In the end the 'consumption so weakened him' that he was forced to give up officiating altogether and became a mere 'hearer'.[3]

The news, which Joshua Mapletoft brought back to Little Gidding after his visit, was grave. Their old friend was dying. His short time in the parish was drawing to a close.

A visitor to the community, one Edmund Duncon, was sent to Bemerton on their behalf, to assure Herbert of their prayers and to take messages to him. Duncon found Herbert weak, but still conscious and anxious about the health of the Ferrars and their community. They prayed together, 'Mrs. *Herbert* provided Mr. *Duncon* a plain Supper and a clean Lodging and he betook himself to rest.' Duncon had an errand in Bath the next day but promised to return to Herbert a few days later.

When he did, he found Herbert much weaker than before 'and therefore their Discourse could not be long'. Herbert handed Duncon a book to take to Ferrar, which his friend could treat with as he thought fit. It was a book which Herbert had been busy re-writing and re-editing throughout his time at Bemerton. He had added to it many new poems. He had changed the order round. Like the rebuilding of his church, he had carefully ordered the structure of the book. He had rebuilt two churches in his life, so it is hardly surprising that when he rebuilt this book he gave it the title of a building: *The Temple*.[4]

According to Walton, Duncon left Herbert about three weeks before his death.[5] Duncon's place at Herbert's bedside was taken by the faithful Arthur Woodnoth, who came from London to Bemerton 'and never left him, till he had seen him draw his last breath, and clos'd his eyes on his death bed.' Herbert was also visited by the local clergy—especially by his own curates—and officials from Salisbury, but it was mainly his wife, his nieces and Arthur Woodnoth who 'were the sad Witnesses of his daily decay'.[6]

He rallied a little at the end of February, playing his lute and singing some of his poems set to music. The next day he wrote his will, which he dictated to Nathaniel Bostocke, his curate. Bostocke and one of the servants, Elizabeth Burden witnessed the will which named Arthur Woodnoth as executor and Sir John Danvers as overseer.

On Friday 1 March 1633, George Herbert died. He was not quite forty years old.

'HE THAT SINGS ON FRIDAY, WILL WEEPE ON SUNDAY.'
Outlandish Proverbs No.411

Burial and Will

He was buried on Sunday, in a simple, unmarked grave. The 'singing men of Sarum' sang, perhaps honouring a friend as much as a fellow clergyman, for Herbert had surely shared with them in his 'Musick evenings' in Salisbury.

Woodnoth wrote to Ferrar that, 'Vppon friday, about foure a Clock itt pleased God to take vnto his mercy the soule of o^r Deere Deere Brother & frend Mr Harbert—whose body vppon Sunday was buried the more particular passages of his Sicknes Death and buriall I shall giue yo an accoumpt.'[7]

In the meantime, there was the will to execute. Herbert left the bulk of his estate–'all my goods both within doores and without doores both monneys and bookes and howshould stuffe'–to his 'deare wife'. He left legacies to his nieces and 'twenty pounds vnto the poore of this parish to be devided according to my deare wiues discretion'. To Mr Hays he left his copy of 'Lucas Brugensis vppon the Scripture' and to Nathaniel Bostocke he left 'St. Augustines workes'. Both curates received their 'halfe yeares wages aforehand'. The document ends, 'If there be any body els that owe me anything else of old debt I forgiue them.'[8]

Woodnoth called Herbert's will, 'the most imperfect act' he ever did, but it did not seem to present him with much difficulty, despite his forebodings. Only a few days later, on 12 March, Arthur proved the will in London.[9]

Herbert had been vicar of the little church of St Andrews for just under three years, years of fulfilment after years of frustration and indecision. Death came to him as no surprise, and even allowing for the over-statement and sanctification of Walton's account, he appears to have been fully prepared for his end. God had brought him through. 'I alwaies fear'd sickness more then death' he had once written to his mother and his poems echo this sentiment. To Herbert, sickness was always seen as an imprisonment. Death, however, was a release.

21

1633-1655

Little Gidding, Montgomery, Chelsea

'A MAN'S DESTINY IS ALWAYES DARK.'
Jacula Prudentum No.1180

Evacuation of Bemerton

'To morrow or Wed[n]esday I suppose M[rs] Herbert will remoue
to her mothers. Two Neeces M[r] Herbert Had living w[th] him for
whose sakes I suppose He was moued to inioyn my imploym[t]...'[1]
Arthur Woodnoth's letter to Nicholas Ferrar written only four
days after Herbert's death, gives an indication of the speed of
events. Within a few days Jane Herbert had left the rectory she
had only known for a few years, dismissed the servants, packed
all her goods and moved back to the family home at Baynton.

The Vaughan sisters, once again on the move, presented
Arthur with a problem. His letter to Ferrar asked for his help in
an emergency: 'If they cannot to there satisfaction be acomodated
wth a convenient place for a while or longer yo[u] will pleas to lett
them com to Gidding.'[2]

Among the responsibilities Woodnoth had in the days following Herbert's death was the preservation of his literary work.
Along with various manuscripts, including *The Country Parson*
and *Outlandish Proverbs*, there must also have been a mass of
personal and private papers. Unfortunately, hardly any of these
personal documents have been preserved. Amy Charles points out
that not a single letter to Herbert has survived. It is inconceivable
that he did not keep some of his correspondence, especially since
he was friendly with some of the most eminent men of the day.

Most likely, the papers were destroyed in the Civil War, when
both Highnam House, where Jane Danvers then lived, and Little
Gidding were looted by Parliamentary forces. Walton records that

Jane Herbert *'preserv'd many of Mr.* Herberts *private Writings, which she intended to make publick; but they, and* Highnam *house, were burnt together, by the late rebels and so lost to posterity.'*[3]

Certain manuscripts, of course, did survive. The manuscript which Edmund Duncon took back to Little Gidding was the collection of poems that was eventually to be published under the title *The Temple*. During his years at Bemerton, Herbert had obviously been busy rearranging and adding to the earlier collection. As soon as Duncon delivered the manuscript into his hands, Ferrar realised the value of the collection of poetry. His brother records that 'when N.F. had many & many a time read over, & embraced & kissed again & again, he sayd, he could not sufficiently admire it, as a rich Jewell, & most worthy to be in ye hands and hearts of all true Christians, that feared God, & loved the Church of England.'[4]

By sending the manuscript of his poems to Ferrar, Herbert had appointed him as a sort of unofficial literary executor. Certainly Ferrar believed so.[5] Within three weeks copies had been made for private circulation.[6] Then a better copy was sent to Cambridge to be licensed for printing. Initially, as we have seen, there were some objections of the censors to overcome. Ferrar, however, refused to remove the lines from the text and in the end the authorities' opposition crumbled. The links between Herbert and Cambridge were still strong, and it was the University printers whom Ferrar proposed should print the works of their late Orator.[7] The book appeared in October 1633, a few months after Herbert's death. Ferrar himself wrote the preface. All in all, the speed of publication was a considerable feat, considering it had to be copied from Herbert's original manuscript and then set at the printers, which in those days was a laborious task.

The manuscript known as *B* has been identified as the copy made at Little Gidding to be sent to the publishers. It appears to be the work of Ferrar's nieces, Anna and Mary Collet. The title and epigraph was added in Ferrar's own hands, which naturally raises the question: Was it Herbert's own title? Amy Charles argues persuasively that it is unlikely Herbert would have chosen this title for himself. It is not impossible, however. Herbert was keenly aware, as were most men of his age, of Old Testament typology. *The Temple* may well have been Herbert's idea to set the sixteenth-century church in the context of the great flow of human history; the Church of England was still the Temple of God. Herbert's poems are rich in allusions to Old Testament types. It may be that *The Temple* had a similar appeal for him.[8] Without the interim copy, the revised version of *W* that Herbert sent from his deathbed, we shall never know if the title was Ferrar's or Herbert's.

Either way, *The Temple* was an immediate sell-out. Indeed, in October 1633, the same month that it was published, Joshua Mapletoft wrote to Ferrar complaining that the publishers had underestimated the popularity of the book:

> Touching Mr Herbert's booke it hath ye most generall approbation y^t I haue knowne any as well it deserues I haue been importuned by diuerse friends for som of y^m London affords none & complaint at Cambridge y^t so few coppyes were printed. If you haue store I shalbe beholding for such a supply as you may afford.[9]

A second edition was printed in the same year and another nine editions in the next fifty years. Few books were to have such an influence on their generation.

HE THAT WILL NOT HAVE PEACE, GOD GIVES HIM WARRE.'
Outlandish Proverbs No.729

The Following Years

Like Herbert, Nicholas Ferrar never had a robust constitution. By the summer of 1637 he was seriously ill. According to his brother, he had long foreseen the troubled times that were to come to the country. In the 1630s when the tenants of the farms at Little Gidding asked for a further fifteen years lease at the same rent, John Ferrar refused. Nicholas, however, intervened and offered them ten years, saying 'they might all have cause to thank God if they could enjoy things in quiet for so long, which he doubted.'[10]

On 3 November 1637 his condition worsened. He died exactly a month later, on Advent Sunday. 'I tell you,' he had said to his brother, 'that you may be forewarned and prepare for it, there will be sad times come, and very sad.'[11] He was not wrong. When the Parliamentarians came to power, the community at Little Gidding was an immediate target, since it had long been suspected of being an 'Arminian Nunnery'. All the papers were burned, the buildings ransacked and the family evicted. Ferrar's dream was reduced to a pile of smouldering rubble and a few fragments of charred paper.

The years after Herbert's death were not only hard for religious people like the Ferrars; they were hard for his family and for his country. In some ways, Herbert's death spared him much pain. He loved England as much as he loved the English Church. His death saved him from the prospect of England tearing itself apart. Families were split asunder: father fought son and brother fought brother, and no family was more torn than the Herberts.

'MARRY A WIDDOW BEFORE SHE LEAVE MOURNING.'
Outlandish Proverbs No.252

Jane Herbert

After George's death, Jane, who was still a young woman, returned to live with her mother. After some six years, she remarried: 'Thus she continued mourning, till time and conversation had so moderated her sorrows, that she became the happy wife of Sir Robert Cook of Highnam in the County of Gloucester Knight,' wrote Walton. According to Walton, however, she could never forget her three years with her saintly first husband. 'Yet she would even to him [Sir Robert] often take occasion to mention the name of Mr. George Herbert, and say, That name must live in her memory, till she put off her mortality.'[12] How Sir Robert responded to this repetitious adulation of his predecessor, Walton does not record.

Jane bore Sir Robert a daughter. In the conflict, Sir Robert fought on the side of the Royalists. In 1642, in a letter to his cousin Sir Robert Harley, he talks bravely of relieving the siege at Bampton Castle, but it was not to be. He died in June 1643. His home at Highnam was burnt by Cromwell's troops, an act which according to Walton destroyed the writings of Herbert preserved by his wife. Jane outlived her second husband by eighteen years. She died on 22 November 1661.[13]

'THE LIFE OF MAN IS A WINTER WAY.'
Outlandish Proverbs No.914

George's Brothers

The rebellion split apart many families, not least the Herbert family. Edward, who had just cause to hate the court, attempted to remain neutral in an environment hostile to anyone who did not nail their colours to the mast. As one pamphlet declared, 'neutrality is malignancy'.[14]

When forced to decide, he was on the King's side. He even joined Charles on his ill-fated expeditions to Scotland in 1639 and 1640, in the war against the Covenanters. In the Long Parliament of 1642, it was Edward who had to stand up in the Lords and read out the warrant for the arrest of the five members.[15] Indeed, in one occasion in 1642 he was even arrested and put in the tower for a few days for a remark deemed to be too favourable to the King.[16]

Mainly, however, he spoke out in favour of moderation. Edward, who had never had much time for any organised religion, now had to stand and watch what organised religion could really do if it tried. Time was taking its toll on the erstwhile soldier and gallant. He was losing his sight and was increasingly ill. He returned to Wales, realising, perhaps, that this was one duel he could never win. His wife had been buried at Montgomery eight years earlier. His friends and fellow braves of former years had died, including Thomas, the adventurous youngest brother, who had never gained the preferment he thought he deserved. After some time acting as deputy to Henry as Master of the Revels, Thomas appears to have spent most of his later years writing 'satiric and scurrilous verse'.[17]

Thomas died in 1643. The following year, bitterly alone, Edward wrote to Henry, 'And let me assure you, I finde myselfe grown older this one yeare than in fifty-nine yeares before... And here I must remember that of all of us, there remains now but you and I to brother it.' On Wednesday 4 September 1644, Montgomery Castle was surrendered to the Parliamentary forces without a shot being fired.[18]

Wales, which was predominantly Royalist, never forgave 'the delivery of the Castle of Montgomery to the enemy by that treacherous Lord of Chirbury'.[19] Succeeding commentators—

especially Edward's various Victorian editors and critics—have continued to vilify him as a turncoat, but one can hardly blame him. He had spent his life trying to promote the King's honour with scant reward for it. He was old, near blind and ill. He had been woken at midnight to find his home besieged by a large Parliamentary force. His beloved castle, with the library which was so precious to him, was under attack. The war was also clearly a religious war—he had always said that religion was a cause of strife. As R.D.Bedford has written, 'Self-preservation in the face of a kind of absurdity was hardly a treachery.'[20]

Edward was escorted to London, where he persuaded the Parliamentary authorities that he had always been on their side and regained his goods and property which had been sequestered because of his supposedly Royalist sympathies. He was granted a pension, but the remainder of his life was lived in relative poverty, pursuing his academic interests and alienated from his pro-Royalist sons.[21]

He died in August 1648. On his death-bed he asked to receive the sacraments from Bishop John Usher, Primate of Ireland. When the bishop arrived, Edward prepared to receive the sacrament by saying 'if there was good in anything 'twas in that, or if it did no good 'twould doe no hurt'. 'The Primate refused it,' said Aubrey, 'for which many blamed him.' Edward then turned his head to the other side and 'expired very serenely.'[22]

Of all the brothers, only Henry survived the conflict, returning in triumph at the Restoration to once again take up the reins as Master of Revels. In his later life, admittedly, he became somewhat ambitious, pressing the case for the Master of Revels to have more and more control over books and plays. Alone among the brothers, he had always been immensely skilled at acquiring money—mostly through the wide range of fees that he charged theatre companies. He died in 1673 at the age of 79.

"'TIS HARD TO BE WRETCHED, BUT WORSE TO BE KNOWNE
SO.'
Outlandish Proverbs No.577

Sir John Danvers

If Edward was viewed as a traitor, that is nothing to the obloquy
heaped on the head of Sir John Danvers. Sir John's bitterness
towards the world in general and the Court in particular probably
began with the failure of the Virginia Company in 1624. Subsequent years of financial hardship caused by his own extravagance and expenditure on his gardens did not help matters. He
served in many Parliaments during these years, not only in the
1624 and 1625 Parliaments, but also in those of 1627-1628, where
he represented Oxford University.

From about 1630 onwards he was struggling with debt (perhaps earlier if Arthur Woodnoth's appointment is any indication).
His second wife, Elizabeth died in 1636. He was an absentee
landlord, but even this he failed at, for he was repeatedly fined for
failing to attend the meetings of the Manor Court at Canning
Canonicorum where he owned some farmland.[23] His sole concern
was his ever-expanding gardens.

Perhaps it was with old grievances in his mind that he refused
to contribute to the King's expedition against Scotland. In 1639,
he was elected MP for Oxford University for the fifth time, and
served in the Short Parliament. His Parliamentary sympathies
never wavered and in 1642 he took up arms for their cause. He
was still desperate for money, so much so that in 1643 he even
challenged the terms of his brother's will, in which Henry
Danvers left his estate to his daughters. Sir John's suit failed, but,
by using his Parliamentary contacts, he was apparently given
some portion of the money.

At the end of the war, in July 1649, he was appointed to the
commission to try the King. He was the only member of the
commission whom the King knew. The following February he
signed the death warrant. Aubrey accuses Danvers of acting out
of purely pecuniary motives:

> Sir John was a great friend of the King's partie and a
> Patron of distressed and cashiered Cavaliers. But to
> revenge himselfe of his sister, the Lady Gargrave, and to

ingratiate himself more with the Protector to null his
brother, Earl of Danby's Will he, contrary to his owne
naturall inclination, did sitt in the High Court of Justice at
the King's Triall.[24]

Clarendon records a somewhat bleaker view of Danvers and
the way he was used by Cromwell and his compatriots:

Being neglected by his brother, and having by a vain
expense in his way of living contracted a vast debt which
he knew not how to pay, and being a proud, formal, weak
man, between being seduced and a seducer, he became so
far involved in their counsels that he suffered himself to be
applied to their worst offices, taking it to be a high honour
to sit upon the same bench with Cromwell, who employed
and contemned him at once: nor did that party of
miscreants look upon any [man] in the Kingdom with that
scorn and detestation as they did upon Danvers.[25]

It is a chilling, almost Stalinistic picture. In the end, even his
Puritan paymasters discarded him and he was obliged to fly the
country under suspicion of having plotted to kill Cromwell.[26]
Eventually he managed to return to England, where he spent his
last days at his beloved Chelsea, no doubt brushing his hat against
the aromatic shrubs and herbs and remembering the days when
he walked the gravel paths with Donne and Aubrey and Bacon
and Herbert. He died on 16 April 1655. Even today, you will find
him listed in books as Sir John Danvers, *Regicide*.

22

Home

'GOD IS AT THE END, WHEN WE THINKE HE IS FURTHEST
OFF IT.'
Outlandish Proverbs No.598

Epilogue

In his final three years at Bemerton, George Herbert truly found
his place. The indecision and disappointment that had tormented
him for so long was a thing of the past. He had found a home in
more than one sense. He had a wife, a family and most of all, a
vocation. Indeed, so fitting was the role of priest that one has to
constantly remind oneself that he spent less than three years
serving in the little church of St Andrews.

Before he came home, however, he had first to become home-
less. Like Joseph in the Bible, he had to lose his identity in order
to find it. All his life, Herbert wanted fame and renown. He
sought it at university, at court, perhaps even at Parliament. In
the end, ironically, he became famous through the very act of
renouncing fame. In order to become something, he had to
choose first to become nothing.

In the end, God was there. In the light of this final fulfilment,
questions about whether or not Herbert always wanted to be a
priest, whether he only turned to it in desperation, or whether he
could never quite make up his mind, become somewhat second-
ary. Yet still we ask them, because we all have the same desire
that Herbert had – the desire to discover order and meaning. We
may look down on Walton for his lack of accuracy and his habit of
invention, but we all play the same game. Every biographer tries
to impose a pattern.

Herbert himself would have done no different. He believed

that life, like a poem, had a structure and a meaning. His love of order and ritual, even the way in which he made poems look like wings, were all part of the same impulse; the desire to discover order beneath a bewildering and confusing world, to see the pattern that God was creating. There were, to be sure, times when he could not understand what God was doing, but there were never any times when he thought that God was not doing anything at all.

This may seem to some a naïve and foolish delusion, but whether we like it or not, it is a view that informs all Herbert's work. At the core of his poetry was his belief that God's involvement with his world gave everything significance, even the meandering movements of a man's life. As Summers wrote:

> Puns, music, love, joy, history, law, farming, business, medicine, the Court, the windows of the Church, the way a bird drinks, the sufferings of the poet and the sufferings of Christ on the cross, all could be used in his poems, not because the poet created their significancies, but because God created them significant. 'Invention' was the Poet's most important task, but Herbert understood the word to mean the discovery of God's truth.[1]

In this sense, Herbert truly 'invented' his own life. He did not turn his life into a pattern, but instead discovered the pattern which had lain there all the time.

'The Church' section of *The Temple* ends with a series of six poems about the end of man's life. It is significant, though, that Herbert did not end his collection of poems with 'A Wreath', or 'Death', or 'Dooms Day', or 'Judgement', or even 'Heaven', but with 'Love (III)'. In the context of the other poems, the subject matter of 'Love' is clear: it is the story of a man entering paradise. Unworthy, sinful, confused, even scared, he is welcomed by Jesus and ushered into the room that he has prepared for him. His journey is over. He has reached the true home at last.

> Love bade me welcome: yet my soul drew back
>   Guiltie of dust and sinne.
> But quick-ey'd Love, observing me grow slack
>   From my first entrance in,

Drew nearer to me, sweetly questioning,
       If I lack'd any thing.
A guest, I answer'd, worthy to be here:
       Love said, You shall be he.
I the unkinde, ungratefull? Ah my deare,
       I cannot looke on thee.
Love took my hand, and smiling did reply,
       Who made the eyes but I?
Truth, Lord, but I have marr'd them. let my shame
       Go where it doth deserve.
And know you not, sayes Love, who bore the blame?
       My deare, then I will serve.
You must sit down, sayes Love, and taste my meat:
       So I did sit and eat.

Main Sources

The following abbreviations have been used in the notes to this book:

Aubrey   *Aubrey's Brief Lives*, ed. Oliver Lawson Dick, London 1958

Charles   Amy Charles, *A Life of George Herbert*, Cornell University Press, 1977

GHJ   *The George Herbert Journal*

Hutchinson   *The Works of George Herbert*, ed. F.E. Hutchinson, London, 1945 ed.

Life   Edward Herbert, *The Life of Edward, First Lord Herbert of Cherbury, written by himself.* Ed J.M. Shuttleworth, OUP, 1976

LST   *Like Season'd Timber–New Essays on George Herbert* ed. Edmund Miller and Robert DiYanni, New York, 1987

Maycock   Alan Maycock, *Nicholas Ferrar of Little Gidding*, SPCK, London, 1938

Patrides   C.A. Patrides, ed., *George Herbert–The Critical Heritage*, London, 1983

Summers   Joseph H. Summers, *George Herbert: His Religion and his Art*, London, 1954

Walton   Izaak Walton, *The Life of Mr. George Herbert*, 1670; 1675. I am quoting from Walton's revised edition, published in 1675.

Notes

CHAPTER ONE

1. John Donne, 'Sermon of Commemoration of the Lady Danvers, late wife of Sir John Danvers, Preach'd at Chelsey, where she was lately buried.' In, *Sermons of John Donne* Vol VIII, edited by Simpson & Pottle, California, 1956, p.61
2. Walton, p.268
3. Donne, p.63
4. *ibid* p.86
5. *ibid* pp.90-91

CHAPTER TWO

1. Patrides, p.3
2. Life, pp.8-9
3. Robert Codrington, 'On Herberts Poems' Bodleian MS Eng. poet. f.27, p. 296 quoted in Patrides, p.63
4. Kenneth Mason, *George Herbert—Priest and Poet*, SLG Press, Oxford, 1980, p.1
5. For a more detailed discussion of the changes in critical opinion see Eugene D. Hill, *Edward, Lord Herbert of Cherbury*, Boston, 1987, pp.104-107
6. *ibid* p.104

CHAPTER THREE

1. *Leland's Itinerary in Wales* ed. Lucy Toulmin Smith. London, 1906, p.11
2. Walton, p.262
3. J.D.K.Lloyd 'Where was George Herbert Born?' Arch Cambrensis 118, 1969, p.140
4. *ibid* p.141
5. Nicholas Ashton and Paul Garwood, *The Excavation of Post-medieval Structures at Plas Du, Montgomery 1980-82*, Archaeologica Cambrensis Vol CXXXIV, pp.190-191
6. Life, pp.3-4
7. Hill, p.1
8. Charles, p.22
9. Life, p.3
10. *ibid* p.3
11. *ibid* p.3
12. *ibid* p.2
13. *ibid* p.3
14. *ibid* p.2
15. Bettie Anne Doebler & Retha M. Warnicke, *Magdalene Herbert Danvers & Donne's Vision of Comfort, GHJ*, Vol. 10: Fall 1986/Spring 1987 p.6
16. Charles, pp.25-26
17. Life, p.11
18. *ibid* p.14
19. *ibid* p.15
20. *ibid* p.36
21. Charles, pp.48-49
22. *ibid* pp.29-30
23. Life, p.15
24. J.P.Kenyon, *The Stuarts*, London 1958, Fontana ed. p.17

CHAPTER FOUR

1. Hill, p.2
2. George Held, *Brother Poets: The Relationship between Edward and George Herbert*, in *LST*, pp.22-23
3. *ibid* p.23
4. Life, p.16
5. *ibid* p.7
6. Charles, p.33
7. *ibid* p.33
8. Life, p.16
9. Nicholas Fitzherbert, *Oxoniensis in Anglia Academia Desciptio*,

1602 Trans. from the Latin by Jan Morris in *The Oxford Book of Oxford*, p.67

10. Paul Hentzner, *A Journey into England in 1598* trans. Horace Walpole, in Morris, *The Oxford Book of Oxford* p.66
11. Walton, pp.266-267
12. John Carey, *John Donne, Life, Mind and Art*, New Edition, London, 1990 pp.16-17
13. Charles, p.34
14. Carey, p.57

CHAPTER FIVE

1. Life, p.35
2. F.P.Wilson, *The Plague in Shakespeare's London*, OUP, 1927, p.215
3. J. Hurstfield, *John Norden's View of London, 1600*, London Topographical Record XXII, 1965, p.6
4. Maycock, p.6
5. Hurstfield, p.6
6. F.N.Macnamara, *Memorials of the Danvers Family (of Dauntsey and Culworth)* London, 1895, pp.287-288
7. John Stow, *A Survey of London, 1603*, ed. Charles Lethbridge Kingsford, 1971, Vol II, p.95
8. *ibid* pp.95-96
9. *ibid* p.100
10. *ibid* p.98
11. Daniel W. Doerksen, 'Magdalen Herbert's London Church', Notes & Queries, 34, 1987, p.303
12. *ibid* p.304
13. F.Barker & P. Jackson, *The History of London in Maps*, London, 1990
14. Ralph Hyde, *The A-Z of Georgian London*, London, 1981
15. See, Amy Charles, 'Mrs Herbert's Kitchen Booke', English Literary Rennaissance IV (Winter 1974) pp.164-173
16. Charles, pp.38-39
17. *ibid* p.38
18. Life, p.36
19. Charles, p.43
20. Donne, *A Sermon of Commemoration*, p.86
21. Charles, p.43
22. Life, p.8 ff.
23. Charles, p.47
24. *ibid* pp.47-48
25. Life, p.36

CHAPTER SIX

1. G.M.Trevelyan, *History of England*, London 1926, p. 327
2. De Maisse, *A Journal of All that was Accomplished...*, ed. G.B.Harrison and R.A.Jones, 1931, pp.25-26, cited in Hurstfield, *John Norden's View of London, 1600*, p.11
3. Christopher Hill, *The Century of Revolution 1603-1714*, 2nd ed. London, 1980, p.25
4. Hurstfield, p.13
5. Life, p.37
6. Christopher Morris, *The Tudors*, London 1955. Fontana ed. pp.147-148
7. J.P.Kenyon, *The Stuarts*, pp.32-33
8. Life, p.37
9. 'T.M.' *The True Narrative of the Entertainment of His Royal Majesty* (1603) quoted in Wilson, *The Plague in Shakespeare's London*, p.88
10. Wilson, p.88
11. *ibid* pp.29-30
12. *ibid* pp.100-102
13. *ibid* pp.92-3
14. Charles, p.49
15. *ibid* p.52
16. Hacket, quoted in Florence Higham, *Lancelot Andrewes*, London, 1952, pp.30-31
17. *ibid* p.30
18. Aubrey, p.7
19. A.G.Hyde, *George Herbert and His Times*, London, 1905, p.30
20. *ibid* p.31
21. John Sargeaunt, *Annals of Westminster School*, London, 1898, cited in Hyde, p.33

22. Hyde, p.35
23. *ibid* p.36

CHAPTER SEVEN

1. Life, p.39
2. *ibid* pp.39-40
3. Florence Higham, *Lancelot Andrewes*, p.44
4. Charles, p.55
5. Life, p.11
6. Carey, *John Donne, Life, Mind and Art* pp.59-60
7. *ibid* p.62
8. Walton, p.268
9. *ibid* p.96
10. John Donne, *Poetical Works*, ed. H.J.C. Grierson, OUP, 1912, p.92
11. Carey, p.68
12. Donne, *op cit* p.93
13. Aubrey, p.81
14. *ibid* p.81
15. Donne, p.88
16. Macnamara, *Memorials of the Danvers Family*, p.293
17. *ibid* pp.287-282
18. Aubrey, p.81
19. *ibid* p.9

CHAPTER EIGHT

1. Thomas Plume, ed. *A Century of Sermons...Preached by...John Hacket*, London, 1675, p.v
2. Charles, p.55
3. G.M. Trevelyan, *Trinity College, An Historical Sketch*, Cambridge, 1972, p.49
4. Charles, pp.66-67
5. *ibid* p.67 n.1
6. John Steegman, *Cambridge*, 5th ed. Revised, London, 1954, p.9
7. *ibid* pp.19-21
8. Hyde, *George Herbert and His Times*, p.41
9. Charles, p.55
10. Hyde, pp.41-42
11. Trevelyan, p.24
12. Steegman, pp.70-71
13. Summers, p.31
14. Trevelyan, pp.31-32

15. Maycock, p.18
16. Trevelyan, p.15
17. Maycock, p.19
18. Thomas Plume, ed., p.v-vi
19. Maycock, p.19
20. *ibid* p.29
21. Hutchinson, p.363
22. Summers, p.33. The Standard edition of Edward's verse is *Poems of Edward, Lord Herbert of Cherbury*, ed. G.C. Moore Smith, London, 1923. Henry's work is analysed in Amy Charles, *Sir Henry Herbert: The Master of Revels as Man of Letters*, Modern Philology, 80, 1982-83, pp.1-12. No-one has bothered to analyse Charles's only known verse, a Latin quatrain which appears in Dr Zouch's *The Dove* (see Sydney Lee, ed. *The Life of Edward Herbert*, p.21 n.3)
23. Hutchinson, p.363
24. *ibid* p.206
25. Edmund Gosse, *Life and Letters of Donne*, 2 vols, London, 1899, ii, p.346
26. Hutchinson, p.79, 'Deniall'.
27. *ibid* p.166, 'The Quidditie', 11.36-38
28. Summers, p.32
29. Hutchinson, p.xxv
30. Maycock, p.13
31. *ibid* p.17
32. *ibid* p.20
33. *ibid* p.117
34. Charles, p.113
35. *ibid* p.71
36. *ibid* p.71
37. Hutchinson, p.xxvii
38. Simonds D'Ewes, *The Autobiography and Correspondence*, ed. J.O. Halliwell, London, 1845, I 106, 121, cited in Charles, p.97
39. Hutchinson, xxvii
40. Steegman, p.26
41. Trevelyan, p.27
42. Charles, p.102
43. Trevelyan, p.25
44. Hutchinson, p.363
45. *ibid* p.364

46. *ibid* p.364
47. *ibid* p.365

CHAPTER NINE

1. Hutchinson, pp.369-370
2. *ibid* p.370
3. Walton, p.272-273
4. Hutchinson, p.370.
5. Epistolae, XVII Ad. R. Creighton, Hutchinson, p.470. The translation is from *Complete Works of George Herbert*, ed. A.B. Grosart, 3 vols, privately printed, 1874, pp.475-476. As far as I am aware, Grosart is the only person who has translated Herbert's Latin orations and letters
6. Patrides, p.57
7. Grosart, p.449
8. *ibid* p.451
9. *ibid* p.433
10. *ibid* p.439
11. *ibid* pp.457-458. Interestingly, the letter to Bacon contains echoes of the letter George sent to his step father. 'But alas Sir, what is that to those infinite Volumes of Divinity, which yet every day swell, and grow bigger' (Letter III, Mar 18 1617, Hutchinson, p.365). 'Thou seest the multitude of books swelling day by day, especially in theology, on which subject if the books were piled one upon another... it is likely that they would climb up to that place where knowledge itself appertains' (Letter to Francis Bacon, Jan 29, 1620, Grosart, p.460)
12. *ibid* pp.470-471
13. Hutchinson, pp.432-434 and p.435
14. See, Ted-Larry Pebworth, *George Herbert's Poems to the Queen of Bohemia: A Rediscovered Text and a New Edition*, English Language Review, 1979, pp.108-120

15. Leicester Bradner, *New Poems by George Herbert: The Cambridge Latin Gratulatory of 1613*, Rennaissance News, Autumn 1962, 208-211.
16. Maycock, p.40
17. Pebworth, p.112
18. Charles, pp.92-93
19. Walton, p.274
20. Hutchinson, p.588
21. *The Latin Poetry of George Herbert, A Bilingual Edition*, trans. Mark McCloskey and Paul R. Murphy, Ohio, 1965, p.3
22. Charles, p.79
23. Charles, p.78 ff. Amy Charles analysis of the two ms. copies of the Temple, and her dating of Herbert's poetry is the best work on the subject. She has also edited two facsimile reproductions of the manuscripts
24. Hutchinson, p.476
25. *ibid* p.6
26. *ibid* p.482
27. *ibid* p.366
28. *ibid* p.196

CHAPTER TEN

1. Hutchinson, p.580
2. Charles, pp.99-100
3. Basil Willey, *Lord Herbert of Cherbury: A Spiritual Quixote of the Seventeenth Century*, Essays & Studies, Vol 27. 1942, pp.23-24
4. Eugene D. Hill, *Edward, Lord Herbert of Cherbury*, Boston, 1987, p.5
5. *ibid* p.7
6. *ibid* p.8
7. Life, p.32
8. Willey, p.25
9. R.D. Bedford, *The Defence of Truth, Herbert of Cherbury and the Seventeenth Century*, Manchester, 1979, p.4
10. *ibid* p.4
11. Hill, p.6
12. George Held, 'Brother Poets: The Relationship between Edward and George Herbert' in *LST*, p.32

13. Edward Herbert, *De Veritate*, trans. Meyrick H. Carré, Bristol, 1937, p.268
14. Hill, p.31
15. Herbert, *De Veritate*, p.75
16. Hutchinson, p.256
17. *ibid* p.xl
18. Edward Herbert, *De Religione Laici* Edited and Trans. Harold R. Hutcheson. New Haven, Yale University Press, 1944, p.123
19. Life, p.8
20. *ibid* p.8
21. *ibid* p.8
22. Hutchinson, p.582
23. Charles, p.93
24. Hutchinson, p.372-373
25. *ibid* p.373
26. Charles, p.93
27. Life, p.9
28. *ibid* pp.9-10
29. *ibid* p.11
30. Kenyon, *The Stuarts*, p.51
31. *ibid* p.57
32. Hutchinson, p.600
33. Christopher Hill, *Society and Puritanism in Pre-Revolutionary England*, London, 1986, p.42
34. Life, p.10
35. Grosart, *Complete Works of Herbert*, p.397
36. Hutchinson, p.419, trans. in Summers, p.41
37. Grosart, pp.403-404
38. *ibid* p.405
39. S.R.Gardiner, *History of England 1603-42*, vii, pp.266-7.
40. E.M. Albright, *Dramatic Publication in England, 1580-1640*, London, 1927, p.165

CHAPTER ELEVEN

1. Charles, p.106
2. Diana Benet, *Herbert's Experience of Politics and Patronage in 1624*, in *GHJ*, Vol 10. Nos 1 & 2. Fall 1986/Spring 1987, p.36
3. Charles, p.107
4. Kenyon, *The Stuarts*, p.56
5. Donne, *A Sermon of Commemoration*, p.86
6. P.R.O., MS SP 14/97, quoted in Doerksen, *Magdalene Herbert's London Church*, pp.302-305
7. *ibid* pp.302-305
8. Bodl. Aubrey MS. 2, fol. 53 quoted in Charles, pp.62-63
9. Aubrey, p.81
10. Charles, p.62
11. Bodl. Aubrey MS. 2, fols. 55-57. Quoted in Charles, p.64
12. Aubrey, p.81
13. Maycock, pp.69-70
14. Amy Charles, 'Spiritual Edification' in *LST*, pp.2-3
15. Maycock, p.71
16. *ibid* p.72
17. Charles, 'Spiritual Edification', p.3
18. Hutchinson, p.278
19. Maycock, p.77
20. *ibid* p.90
21. *ibid* p.96
22. *ibid* p.100
23. Summers, pp.42-43
24. B. Blackstone, ed. *The Ferrar Papers*, Cambridge, 1938, pp.22-23
25. Barnabas Oley, *A Prefatory View of the Life of Mr Geo. Herbert* in Patrides, p.79
26. Walton, p.319
27. Amy Charles, 'Spiritual Edification', p.7
28. Hutchinson, p.277
29. *ibid* p.xxx
30. Charles, pp.110-111

CHAPTER TWELVE

1. Charles, p.113
2. *ibid* p.112
3. Summers, p.38
4. Maycock, p.120
5. Thomas Richards, *Two Studies in the History of the Diocese of Bangor*, Archaeologica Cambrensis, LXXX, 7th Series, Vol. 5, 1925, p.47. George's successor in the post had so many different churches he was summoned to answer charges of 'supine neglecte' in serving the parishioners of Llandinam

6. Kenyon, *The Stuarts*, pp.61-62
7. Maycock, p.111
8. Charles Carlton, *Charles I – The Personal Monarch*, London, 1983, p.71
9. Walton, p.280
10. Walton, p.280
11. Rosemond Tuve, *A Reading of George Herbert*, London, 1952, p.104
12. Hutchinson, p.89, 'The Pearl'
13. *ibid* p.47, 'Affliction (I)'
14. *ibid* p.47, 'Affliction (I)'
15. *ibid* p.89, 'Affliction (IV)'
16. *ibid* p.45, 'Sinne (I)'
17. *ibid* p.95
18. *ibid* p.71
19. Tuve, pp.122-123
20. Hutchinson, p.159, 'Joseph's Coat'
21. N.F., *The Printers to the Reader*, in Patrides, p.60
22. Hutchinson, p.xxxi
23. This is the theory outlined in David Novarr, *The Making of Walton's Lives*, New York, 1958, p.503. The exact time and date is not known for sure. Walton dates it as 'a little before his [Donne's] death', which would be in 1631
24. Steegman, *Cambridge*, p.27
25. Carlton, p.71
26. Roger Lockyer, *Buckingham*, London, 1981, p.321
27. Charles, p.69
28. Patrides, p.57
29. In Honorem Verulemij, trans. Edmund Blunden, in *George Herbert's Latin Poems*, Essays and Studies, XIX, 1934, pp.35-36
30. Hutchinson, p.xxx
31. Charles Whitney, 'Bacon and Herbert as Moderns', in *LST*, pp.231
32. Walton, p.278-279
33. Hutchinson, p.138, 'The Size',

CHAPTER THIRTEEN

1. Life, p.9
2. Amy Charles, 'Sir Henry Herbert: The Master of the Revels as Man of Letters', Modern Philology, 80, 1982-83, p.2
3. *ibid* pp.2-3
4. E.M. Albright, *Dramatic Publication in England, 1580-1640*, p.55
5. Held, 'Brother Poets', in *LST*, p.23
6. Life, p.9
7. Charles, p.120
8. *ibid* p.120
9. Hutchinson, p.xxxi
10. Charles, p.121
11. *ibid* pp.121-122
12. Hutchinson, p.xxxi
13. See letter from Dr. Mary E. Finch, quoted in Charles, pp.123-124
14. Walton, p.282
15. Charles, p.128
16. Blackstone, p.58
17. Maycock, p.274
18. Hutchinson, p.57. 'Employment (I)'
19. *ibid* p.57. 'Employment (I)'
20. Walton, p.288
21. Frank L. Huntley, 'The Williams Manuscript, Edmund Duncon, and Herbert's Quotidian Fever', in *GHJ*, Vol 10. Nos 1 & 2. Fall 1986/Spring 1987, p.25
22. Charles, pp.127-128
23. Matthew 16:24
24. Hutchinson, p.164, 'The Crosse',
25. *ibid* p.164
26. Walton, pp.282-283

CHAPTER FOURTEEN

1. Walton, p.288
2. *The Country Parson*, Chap. XXIII, Hutchinson, p.260
3. *The Country Parson*, Chap. XXIII, Hutchinson, p.261
4. *The Country Parson*, Chap. XXIII, Hutchinson, p.262
5. Hutchinson, p.119, 'Providence',
6. Blackstone, p.59

7. Hutchinson, p.565
8. *ibid* p.565
9. *ibid* p.292
10. *The Country Parson*, Chap. X, Hutchinson, pp.241-242
11. Daniel W. Doerksen, *Magdalen Herbert's London Church*, p.304
12. Donne, pp.86-87
13. Charles, pp.131-132
14. *ibid* p.133, 'Memoriae Matris Sacrum XIV'
15. 'Epitaphium', 'Memoriae Matris Sacrum XIII' in Paul M. Dowling, 'The Muse Displaced: The Architecture of Memoriae Matris Sacrum', in *LST*, p.185
16. 'Memoriae Matris Sacrum II', in *The Latin Poems of George Herbert: A Bilingual Edition*, p.127
17. 'Memoriae Matris Sacrum XVI', trans. Rhonda Blair in *George Herbert's Greek Poetry*, Philological Quarterly, 64, 1985, p.583
18. 'Memoriae Matris Sacrum XVII', *ibid* pp.583-584
19. *The Latin Poems of George Herbert: A Bilingual Edition*, p.139
20. 'Memoriae Matris Sacrum XVII', in Blair, p.584
21. 'Memoriae Matris Sacrum XIX', trans. F.E. Hutchinson. Hutchinson, p.595
22. 'Memoriae Matris Sacrum XVII', in Blair, p.583
23. Charles, p.134
24. Summers, p.213 n.66
25. F.N. Macnamara, *Memorials of the Danvers Family*, p.295
26. N.W. Bawcett, 'New Revels Documents of Sir George Buc and Henry Herbert', Review of English Studies, Vol 35, No.139, 1984, p.321
27. Macnamara, p.295
28. Hutchinson, p.382
29. Walton, p.289
30. *ibid* p.107

CHAPTER FIFTEEN

1. Hutchinson, p.57, 'Employment (I)'
2. *ibid* p.56, 'The Temper (II)'
3. *ibid* p.55, 'The Temper (I)'
4. *ibid* p.60, 'Grace'
5. *ibid* p.61, 'Praise (I)'
6. *ibid* p.90, 'Affliction (IV)'
7. *ibid* p.43, 'Easter-wings'
8. *ibid* p.47, 'Affliction (I)'
9. *ibid* p.47, 'Affliction (I)'
10. *ibid* p.65, 'Church-musick'
11. *ibid* p.51, 'Prayer'

CHAPTER SIXTEEN

1. Walton, p.290
2. Charles, p.144
3. Hutchinson, p.35, 'The Thanksgiving'
4. *ibid* pp.236-237
5. Macnamara, *Memorials of the Danvers Family*, pp.534-535
6. Aubrey, p.137
7. *ibid* p.137
8. Walton, pp.289-290
9. Aubrey, p.137
10. Macnamara, p.535
11. Hutchinson, pp.88-89
12. *ibid* p.xxxi
13. Walton, p.291
14. Hutchinson, p.xxxiv
15. Walton, p.283
16. Hutchinson, pp.xxxiv-xxxv
17. For more information on Davenant, see *The Subscription Book of Bishops Tounson and Davenant 1620-1640*, ed. Barrie Williams, Wiltshire Record Soc. Vol XXXII, 1976
18. Walton, p.293
19. *ibid* p.112
20. Aubrey, p.137
21. Walton, p.298
22. Charles, p.148
23. 'N.F.' 'The Printers to the Reader' in Patrides, p.60
24. Blackstone, pp.58-59
25. Hutchinson, p.379
26. Walton, p.298

CHAPTER SEVENTEEN

1. Hutchinson, p.582
2. *ibid* p.375
3. *ibid* p.375
4. *ibid* pp.375-376
5. Charles, p.155
6. Hutchinson, p.376
7. Herbert G. Wright, 'Was George Herbert the Author of Jacula Prudentum?', RES 11, 1935, p.139
8. *ibid* p.141
9. Hutchinson, p.233, *The Country Parson*, Chap VII, 'The Parson Preaching'
10. Summers, p.96
11. Hutchinson, p.68, 'Trinitie Sunday'
12. *ibid* p.132, 'Paradise'
13. *Poems of Edward, Lord Herbert of Cherbury*, ed. G.C. Moore Smith, London, 1923, pp.47-48. The snappily titled 'Dittie to the tune of *A Che del Quantomio* of Pesarino' also uses the device, pp.26-27
14. Hutchinson, pp.167-168, 'The Sonne'
15. Tuve, *A Reading of George Herbert*, p.138
16. John Dryden, 'MacFlecknoe', 11.203-8, in Patrides, p.137
17. Wrightson, p.210
18. Ida Gandy, *Round About the Little Steeple—The Story of a Wiltshire Parson 1573-1623*, Gloucester, 1989, p.71
19. Charles Stanford, *Joseph Alleine: His Companions and Times*, London, 1861, pp.9-10. Sherfield was so enraged, he smashed the windows with a pikestaff. He was tried in the Star Chamber on 8 Feb 1633. (See, Clifford Davidson, 'George Herbert and Stained Glass Windows', in *GHJ* Vol.12, No.1, Fall, 1988, pp.33-34)
20. Wrightson, p.210
21. *ibid* pp.212-213
22. Gandy, p.70
23. Wrightson, *English Society 1580-1680*, p.209
24. *ibid*
25. *ibid*
26. Matt. 7:20
27. Patrides, p.82
28. Hutchinson, p.224
29. *ibid* p.227, Chap. II, 'The Parson's Life'
30. *ibid* p.228, Chap. II, 'The Parson's Life'
31. *ibid* p.241, Chap. X, 'The Parson in his House'
32. *ibid* p.228, Chap. II, 'The Parson's Life'
33. *ibid* p.231, Chap. VI, 'The Parson Praying'
34. *ibid* pp.228-229, Chap. IV, 'The Parsons Knowledg'
35. *ibid* p.232, Chap. VII, 'The Parson Preaching'
36. *ibid* p.235, Chap. VII, 'The Parson Preaching'
37. *ibid* p.233, Chap. VII, 'The Parson Preaching'
38. *ibid* p.246, Chap. XIII, 'The Parson's Church'
39. *ibid* p.274, Chap. XXXII, 'The Parson's Surveys'
40. *ibid* p.277, Chap. XXXII, 'The Parson's Surveys'
41. *ibid* p.225, Chap. I, 'Of a Pastor'
42. Oley, in Patrides, p.76
43. Hutchinson, p.268, 'The Parson in Contempt'

CHAPTER EIGHTEEN

1. Gene Edward Veith Jr., 'The Religious Wars in George Herbert Criticism: Reinterpreting Seventeenth Century Anglicanism', *GHJ*, Vol. 11 No.2, Spring 1988, p.19
2. Harold H. Kollmeier, 'The Country Parson in Its Time', in *LST*, p.196
3. There is a record, however, of an attempt to publish *The Country Parson* before Oley's edition of 1652. In 1641, Sir Robert Cook, the second husband of Jane

Herbert wrote to Sir Robert Harley to ask his assistance in publishing the book (which, significantly, he referred to, as *The Country Parson*). At the time of writing, the manuscript appears to have been in the hands of one Dr Holdsworth, who had been given it by Arthur Woodnoth. Jane gave her permission for the work to be published, but nothing came of the project. See, Kollmeier, *ibid*, p.193 n.

4. Summers, p.13
5. Ilona Bell, 'Setting Foot into Divinity: George Herbert and the English Reformation', MLQ 38, 1977, p.220
6. Summers, p.35
7. Carlton, Charles I, pp.163-164
8. Hill, *The Century of Revolution*, pp.75-76
9. Summers, pp.57-58
10. Hutchinson, p.170
11. Douglas Bush, *English Literature in the Earlier Seventeenth Century*, Oxford History of English Literature Vol V, p.337
12. Ilona Bell, 'In The Shadow of the Temple', in *LST*, p.261
13. Hutchinson, p.318
14. *ibid* p.196, 'The Church Militant' 11.235-236
15. Dwight Levang, 'George Herbert's "The Church militant" and the Chances of History', Philological Quarterly 36, p.265
16. Veith Jr., p.21
17. Summers, p.53
18. *ibid* p.49
19. Barnabas Oley, *Preface to Herbert's Remains*, cited in Summers, p.49
20. Bell, The Shadow of the Temple, p.279

CHAPTER NINETEEN

1. Hutchinson, p.66, 'Church-Musick'
2. Helen Wilcox, '*Country-Aires* to *Angels Musick*', in *LST*, p.43

3. Hill, p.74
4. Summers, pp.160-161
5. Hutchinson, p.42, 'Easter'
6. Walton, pp.308
7. Aubrey, p.137
8. Gandy, p.71
9. Walton, pp.308-309
10. *ibid* p.104
11. Maycock, p.162
12. *ibid* p.165
13. Hutchinson, p.380
14. Charles, p.170
15. Blackstone, pp.267
16. Hutchinson, p.226, *The Country Parson*, Chap. II, 'Their Diversities'
17. Blackstone, p.267
18. Aubrey, p.137
19. Hutchinson, p.583
20. Vita Sackville-West, *Knole and the Sackvilles*, Fourth ed. 1958, p.67
21. Hutchinson, p.377
22. Sackville-West, p.83
23. Hutchinson, p.583
24. Patrides, p.76

CHAPTER TWENTY

1. Charles, p.126
2. Maycock, p.234
3. Walton, p.313
4. There are many problems with Walton's account, particularly in discrepancies as to who passed the manuscript of *The Temple* to Nicholas Ferrar. Frank L. Huntley postulates the intriguing and totally unprovable theory that Edmund Duncon visited Herbert, not in 1633, but in 1626, when he was at his brother Henry's house and nearly died. The volume given to him would therefore have been the *W* manuscript. See, Frank L. Huntley, 'The Williams Manuscript, Edmund Duncon and Herbert's Quotidian Fever', *GHJ*, pp.23-32
5. Walton, p.322
6. *ibid* p.323
7. Blackstone, pp.276-277

8.   Hutchinson, pp.382-383
9.   *ibid* p.586

CHAPTER TWENTY-ONE

1.   Blackstone, *The Ferrar Papers*,
     p.277
2.   *ibid*
3.   Walton, p.328
4.   Blackstone, p.59
5.   Blackstone, FP no. 550.
6.   Maycock, p.235
7.   Charles, p.181
8.   See Charles, pp.185-186 and
     Tuve, *A Reading of George
     Herbert, passim*
9.   Patrides, p.3
10. Maycock, p.292
11. Maycock, p.293
12. Walton, p.327
13. Hutchinson, p.586
14. Hill, p.15
15. Carlton, p.234
16. R.D.Bedford, *The Defence of
     Truth*, p.7
17. Charles, p.46
18. The account of the surrender of
     Montgomery Castle is told by an
     unidentified author in
     Archaeologica Cambrensis,
     LXXVIII, 7th Series, Vol 3,
     1923, pp.357-359. The castle was
     surrounded at dead of night by
     Sir Thomas Myddleton with 800
     soldiers. The articles of
     surrender were dated 'halfe an
     hour past twelve of the clocke at
     midnight on Thursday the fift
     day of September Anno D'ni,
     1644.'
19. Archaeologica Cambrensis,
     LXXVIII, 7th Series, Vol 3,
     1923, p.359
20. Bedford, p.15
21. Hill, pp.15-16. As Bedford points
     out, however, such
     disagreements were often more
     flexible and forgiveable than later
     critics would like to think.
     Edward's favourite grandson was
     also called Edward and was the
     royalist son of his royalist father,
     Richard. Yet that did not stop
     him marrying the daughter of Sir
     Thomas Middleton, the
     Parliamentarian soldier to whom
     Edward had surrendered
     Montgomery Castle. Clearly
     grudges were not held for long.
     See, R.D.Bedford, *The Defence
     of Truth*, p.18
22. Aubrey, p.135
23. Gandy, *Round About The Little
     Steeple*, pp.45-46
24. Aubrey, p.81. Twenty-six years
     earlier, Herbert, in an oration to
     Charles had said, 'Nothing is
     more useful for a king than
     sometimes not to reign; for this
     cuts off pride, puts to the proof
     the dispositions of the mind,
     dispenses flattery and
     flatterers...' (Grosart, *Complete
     Works*, Vol II, p.412)
25. Clarendon, *History of the Great
     Rebellion and Civil Wars in
     England*, xi. 237 Ed. W Dunn
     Macready, 1888. Vol IV, p.487
26. Macnamara, *Memorials of the
     Danvers Family*, pp.295-296

CHAPTER TWENTY-TWO

1.   Summers, p.185

INDEX